DESTROYING
THE LIE OF THE AGES

**Discovering God's Purpose in
Times of Pain and Grief**

W. EDWARD LONGEST

WINTERS
PUBLISHING

winterspublishing.com

Published by:
Winters Publishing
P.O. Box 501
Greensburg, IN 47240
812-663-4948
www.winterspublishing.com

ISBN: 978-1-954116-16-0

Library of Congress Control Number: 2022948320

What Others are Saying About
Destroying The Lie of the Ages

Having known Bill for more than 20 years, it was a privilege to read this book. His explanation of the "lie of the ages" is simple and yet deep, with great points—and the promise of hope with fortunes restored, even if not before we die, if we choose NOT to believe the "lie of the ages"—along with excellent biblical examples. Most of all, the book is filled with the HOPE we find in Jesus! My favorite quote comes from the chapter about Hezekiah, "The pattern presented by the Lord is to trust God enough to ask in prayer for what you need, and then to trust God enough to act on what you have prayed." May God help us do just that!

—Rev. Phil Reed
Assemblies of God Missionary

I can recommend this inspirational work by Bill Longest wholeheartedly. Herein he aptly tackles one of the most difficult topics that has challenged both the philosopher and the theologian for millennia and he does so with grace and eloquence. Rather than gloss over or ignore the seeming silence of God, the author challenges the deception of Satan and then demonstrates how God works through and in our suffering to offer growth and strength. In so doing, my dear friend has provided us with a refreshing take on this age-old problem of pain and loss, and in so doing, offers a true hope for the one suffering and reassurance for those who may be doubting as they struggle with loss. As one who has dealt with the pain of deep personal loss, I found this book spoke to me on a personal level and can and will encourage anyone who has endured difficult periods in life to read this book and be uplifted in understanding how God works to counter Satan's deception for our good and His glory.

—Dr. Dale R. Meade
Lifelong missionary to Colombia, South America, and
Professor of Missions/Intercultural Studies
Kentucky Christian University
Grayson, Kentucky

Contents

Now to Him who is able to do far more abundantly beyond all that we ask or think, according to the power that works within us, to Him be the glory in the church and in Christ Jesus to all generations forever and ever. Amen (Ephesians 3:20–21 NASB).

❧ **Acknowledgments** ❧

I give heartfelt thanks to my wife, Janelle; my children; Dr. Dale Meade; Phil Reed; my special friend, Dustin Sammons; and to all who provided encouragement and feedback for this project.

The Lord has worked through each of you to make this book better.

Foreword

I have known Bill as a close friend and fellow believer of Jesus Christ for quite a few years. His humble, but vast knowledge of Scripture has always inspired and challenged me to dig deeper into my own faith. Bill has a gentle and caring spirit about him that instantly draws you in, as if you had been friends for a lifetime. A true friendship like this can be hard to find. I am thankful and a finer person because of it. I am so excited that Bill wrote this book, and I have no doubt in my mind that it will impact many lives for the glory of God!

For as long as I have known Bill, he has always lived his life in surrender and servitude to the Lord. To equip Bill to speak on this topic, the Lord has used Bill's personal study in God's Word; four years of study at Cincinnati Bible College; four years as a missionary in Colombia; and his role as lead pastor at Nicholson Valley Christian Church of French Lick, Indiana from 1996 to 1999. This is a man who has devoted his life to studying and understanding the truths of God's Word, and the evidence of this can be clearly seen in his daily living. Bill is a devoted husband to his loving wife, Janelle (married in February of 1990), and is a wonderful role model for his six amazing kids. It is a joy to see so much of Bill's character come to life in their personalities.

The truth is, Bill could not have shared this writing with me at a more crucial time in my life. I had just lost my loving wife, Elizabeth, of fifteen years, to a long, arduous battle with heart failure. I found myself asking, *If God is so good, so loving, and all powerful, why did I have to face loss like this?* If you have ever faced difficult trials or circumstances that have caused you to question God's love for you, then this book is for you! In this work, Bill tackles this tough question by taking an honest and unique look into the character of Jesus, which he exposes as he digs into some of the compelling stories of the Bible. I speak from experience when I say this book will change your life forever.

This truly is a dynamically powerful tool and resource that can help you to regain the right perspectives and achieve victory over the lie of the ages. Bill's simple and genuine approach to this topic is heartfelt and comes from a place of wanting his readers to know the truth that will set them free. The unique and engaging perspective taken on this topic brought me back to a place of understanding God's truth: that He is *for* me and not *against* me—that He really does have my best interests in mind. It truly is Bill's hope and intention to point all to the one true hope that is found in Jesus Christ alone!

Brother in Christ,

Dustin Sammons

∾ **Preface** ∾

Dealing with the questions related to human suffering and pain is something that many authors and theologians have wrestled with through the ages. It certainly is not my intention to cause the reader of this work to believe that I think that I have somehow found or expressed in this work all the answers about the subject. It is also not my intention to lead anyone to think that either I, or this book, are what destroy the lie of the ages.

What then, is my intention? It is simply to explain what the lie of the ages is, and to show how Jesus Christ destroys it forever.

It is not to explain all the reasons why people suffer pain and grief, or to show how to never have any pain and grief (that is not possible in this life). It is also not to encourage people to pursue pain or grief, as though these were somehow desirable. They are not. Rather, it is to state that when we do experience pain or grief, we need to continue to trust that God knows about it, understands it, and still has our best interests at heart. It is simply to encourage the reader to always "trust in the LORD with all your heart, and do not lean on your own understanding" (Proverbs 3:5), and to continue to do this even in times of pain and grief.

Chapter 1

The Lie of the Ages

It is believed that there are more than 6,500 languages in the world, and at the time of this writing, approximately 195 different countries exist. Clearly, this indicates a grand diversity of people roams the planet. There are people of all sorts of shapes, sizes, and ages, yet we all have times when we suffer pain and grief. One question all of humanity shares is, "Why?" Why is there so much pain and grief in our lives? It seems everyone is touched by this common problem.

To make matters worse, we also have a common enemy. The Bible describes this enemy as "… that ancient serpent, who is called the devil and Satan, the deceiver of the whole world— …" (Revelation 12:9). While we are suffering, he whispers to us, *If God is so good, so loving, and all powerful, then why are you suffering this way?* This is what I call the lie of the ages. It is the idea that God does not have our best interests at heart. If He did, then He would not allow such pain and grief to occur in our lives, or so the line goes.

I refer to this idea as the lie of the ages because it was originally presented to the very first two people who lived on the planet. The prototype man and his wife were lovingly created by God and placed in a garden paradise so that they could enjoy perfect fellowship with God and with one another. It was this lie—that God did not have their best interests at heart—that the devil introduced to Eve in the Garden of Eden.

The sacred Scriptures tell us that "… the serpent was more crafty than any other beast of the field that the LORD God had made"

(Genesis 3:1). Based on Revelation 12:9, I take the position that it was the devil (Satan) who spoke to Eve in the form of a serpent as described in Genesis, Chapter 3, and that it was the devil's desire to tempt the first couple to fall into rebellion against God. We know from the teaching of Jesus that the devil operates in the domain of deception (John 8:44), and that God operates in the domain of truth (John 17:17), and so when the devil worked to tempt her, he used a very crafty strategy based on deception.

One thing to notice is that he targeted the pair by attacking an individual rather than confronting them together as a team. He directs his temptation to the woman. The Bible says that at the time Eve ate the fruit she also gave some to her husband who was with her (Genesis 3:6), but it is not mentioned whether Adam was there at the time the devil spoke to her. If he was present for this dialogue, he is strangely quiet.

The first thing the devil does in this conversation is cast doubt on God's Word:

> He said to the woman, "Did God actually say, 'You shall not eat of any tree in the garden?" (Genesis 3:1).

By putting the question to her in this way he is implying either that God never really said this at all, or if He did, then it is an unreasonable commandment. He paints it as though the commandment is too strict by suggesting that they could not eat the fruit from any of the trees, when only one tree was forbidden. This question was designed to cast doubt on whether she really understood what God had said, and on whether she could really trust what God had said at all.

Next, the serpent presents three kinds of lies to Eve. The first is the outright lie. "… You will not surely die" (Genesis 3:4). This is a direct contradiction to what God had stated. God had said that in the day they ate of this fruit they would surely die (Genesis 2:17), but the serpent said that if they ate the fruit they would not surely die. These statements are logical contradictions and cannot both be correct. One of them is consistent with the reality that will take place and one of them is not. That means one of them is true and one of them is false. So, at this point, Eve has two distinct voices saying to her two different things that cannot both be right, and she must decide which voice is to be trusted and obeyed.

The second type of lie presented is the half-truth. This, in a way, is more dangerous, because it is more difficult to figure out which part to believe and which part to reject. The serpent said:

> "For God knows that when you eat of it your eyes will be opened, and you will be like God, knowing good and evil" (Genesis 3:5).

While it was true that by eating the forbidden fruit her eyes would be opened, the serpent does not tell her how this will happen. If she eats the fruit in disobedience to God, she will come to know the difference between good and evil, but what he does not tell her is this will happen by her becoming evil. She will recognize good by viewing it from the outside. She will go into a dark state from which she can never return on her own. He takes a thing that is horrible and presents it as though it is desirable, by leaving out the most important information. Concerning this dialogue, Francis A. Schaeffer comments:

> In a way, there is a half-truth here. Satan's approach has often taken that form ever since. It is true that Eve is indeed going to learn something. If she chooses to disobey and to rebel, she will have what she couldn't have otherwise—an experiential knowledge of evil and its results. So in a way Satan is telling her the truth. But what a useless, horrible knowledge! It is the knowledge of the child whose mother says, "Don't go near that fire because if you do you will get hurt. You will catch fire and be burned." But the little child goes on in disobedience, falls into the fire and spends the next three days dying in agony. The child has learned something that it wouldn't have known experientially if it had listened to the knowledge given by its mother. But what a knowledge! (Schaeffer, p. 81).

The third type is the most subtle, and possibly, the most dangerous of the lies. The serpent frames his comments in a manner that indicates there is something amiss with God's motives for having given the commandment. The lie, in this case, is in the realm of assumptions, rather than being directly stated. The implication is, *God is holding out on you because He is selfish and insecure and does not want anyone to be like Himself. He does not have your best interests at heart.*

This is a crafty and extremely dangerous tactic. The serpent did not state this lie outright, but it was assumed and implied by what he did state. This tactic leaves the lie in the realm of assumptions. Unstated assumptions conveniently dwell beyond the reach of open debate. The statement was that God knew something, but the unstated implication was that because of what He knew, He therefore gave a commandment with intentions that were somehow selfishly motivated, and not really in Adam's or Eve's best interests. The serpent wanted Eve to doubt that God really loved her, which would lead her to believe He did not have good intentions toward her. When the enemy succeeds in causing us to doubt the goodness of God, he also succeeds in tempting us to sin, and many disastrous results follow. After all, why obey a God who does not really love you, and who may not be telling you the whole truth? Eve doubted the intentions of God, and so she ate the fruit.

This is what I am referring to as the lie of the ages, the idea that God does not really have good intentions for us. It is to doubt His love toward us; it is to doubt His goodness. We are especially prone to believe this lie when we suffer pain or grief. "Why would God let this happen?" we ask. The lie seems more believable when people are hurting.

Struggling with this question has led people throughout history to be shaken to the core, and some to even lose their faith in God altogether.

C. S. Lewis, one of the great Christian thinkers of the twentieth century, wrestled with this very question when his wife, Helen Joy Davidman, died in July of 1960. While reflecting on her loss, he wrote:

Meanwhile, where is God? This is one of the most disquieting symptoms. When you are happy, so happy that you have no sense of needing Him, so happy that you are tempted to feel

His claims upon you as an interruption, if you remember yourself and turn to Him with gratitude and praise, you will be—or so it feels—welcomed with open arms. But go to Him when your need is desperate, when all other help is vain, and what do you find? A door slammed in your face, and a sound of bolting and double bolting on the inside. After that, silence. ...

Not that I am (I think) in much danger of ceasing to believe in God. The real danger is of coming to believe such dreadful things about Him. The conclusion I dread is not, "So there's no God after all," but, "So this is what God's really like. Deceive yourself no longer" (Lewis, *A Grief Observed*, pp. 4–5).

Lewis here is speaking from his emotions while grieving, not from the truth, or from his final conclusion on the matter. God's Word declares that He is a very present help in time of trouble (Psalm 46:1), but there are moments it may not seem so, at the time we are grieving. This is precisely when the temptation to believe the lie of the ages is often at its strongest. While Lewis was able to work through his questions and maintain a strong faith in God, there are those who do not. The lie of the ages has taken its toll throughout history and left in its wake some who have completely lost their faith in God.

Yet, it need not be so.

Even though the Lord may not answer all our questions exactly when and how we want Him to, it does not follow that He has left himself without witness. He has addressed quite thoroughly in Scripture the topic of pain and suffering. I believe He has offered several important answers to our deepest questions. It will be the goal of this book to look at some of the answers that He has provided, both by His words and His actions.

We will begin by looking at an example of how Jesus dealt with a small family from the Judean village of Bethany, then progress to God's dealings with a few selected individuals throughout the Scriptures, and conclude with Jesus' own example in experiencing suffering. I think that you will see that the Lord has given by word and by deed more than enough evidence to forever destroy the lie of the ages.

Chapter 2

Jesus' Friends and Their Call for Help

An Introduction to Mary, Martha, and Lazarus

To address the questions that surround the issue of pain and grief and why we sometimes experience them, let us begin by considering the event known to many as the raising of Lazarus. This event is described in the eleventh chapter of the gospel of John. To best understand what happened here, it would be good to know something of the setting and the people involved.

The event occurred in a small village named Bethany. This village was located on the southeastern slope of the Mount of Olives, about two miles east of Jerusalem, as one traveled on the road toward Jericho (Easton, p. 79). Here lived a brother and two sisters, whose names were Lazarus, Mary, and Martha.

We learn from the first three verses of John, Chapter 11, that by the time this event occurred, Jesus had already developed a close friendship with this small family of followers. Verse 5 states, "Now Jesus loved Martha and her sister and Lazarus," and Verse 3 shows that, as they appealed to Jesus for assistance in this event, Martha and Mary described Lazarus as "he whom you love."

Luke, in his gospel, describes an event that helps us understand more concerning the relationship between this family and Jesus. The event is recorded toward the end of Chapter 10, and although Lazarus is not mentioned, it does involve his two sisters.

Now as they went on their way, Jesus entered a village. And a woman named Martha welcomed him into her house. And she had a sister called Mary, who sat at the Lord's feet and listened to his teaching. But Martha was distracted with much serving. And she went up to him and said. "Lord, do you not care that my sister has left me to serve alone? Tell her then to help me." But the Lord answered her, "Martha, Martha, you are anxious and troubled about many things, but one thing is necessary. Mary has chosen the good portion, which will not be taken away from her (Luke 10:38–42).

Here are some conclusions we can draw from what is recorded about this event. We know from John 11:1 that the village mentioned here is Bethany. We know that Martha is at least part owner in a house, and she is mentioned as the one who welcomed Jesus and His disciples into her house. By this time in Jesus' ministry, she was acquainted with Jesus well enough to not only welcome Him into her home, but she referred to Him as "Lord" and looked to Him to direct affairs and solve problems.

We also learn something of the personalities of Mary and Martha here. Mary is described as sitting at Jesus' feet and listening to His teaching. She seemed to be hanging on every word. When Jesus was speaking, she saw it as an opportunity to take in all she could. She does not appear to be a very outspoken person, as there are no recorded words from her in this event. It is easy to picture her as sensitive and quiet, and as a person who valued the Lord's words in such a way that she did not want to miss a thing.

Martha, for her part, comes across as a more action-oriented person. She seems to be the type to make things happen, and to want them to happen in the right way. She is a generous person. She is mentioned here as the one who invited Jesus into her home, and is described as serving, but, according to the text, her serving becomes a distraction. Getting the job done right had grown to be more important than hearing what Jesus had to say, and so the Lord gently corrected her.

Martha also appears to be more vocal, and maybe a bit less sensitive, since she was willing to rebuke her sister. We do not really know for sure whether Martha made this accusation in front of the other guests, or whether it was spoken only to Jesus, but the way the text flows, one gets the impression that it was made in front of all present. If so, then this had to be an embarrassing moment for Mary. Martha was even willing to be somewhat critical of Jesus when she said, "Do you not care that my sister has left me to serve alone? Tell her then to help me" (Luke 10:40). She appears to be used to correcting what is wrong in the world and does not mind telling Jesus how to solve this perceived problem. She comes across with a driving, action-oriented personality.

Martha, though, was also teachable. Her relationship with the Lord was not hindered by His correcting her. We will see later, during the activities surrounding the raising of Lazarus, that she was the first to come out and speak with Jesus and make solid statements of faith concerning His identity as the Messiah.

This event, recorded by Luke, helps to set the stage for us with regard to what happens later with the raising of Lazarus, and gives added insight into the relationship Jesus had with this family from Bethany when that event occurred.

Jesus' Friends Cry for Help

The events I am about to describe took place during the final year of Jesus' earthly ministry, sometime between December and April of that year. John, Chapter 10, relates that Jesus had a rather stirring discussion with the Jewish leaders during the Feast of Dedication (John 10:22–39). During this conversation, He made the claim to be "One with the Father" in such a powerful way that the Jews took up stones to stone Him. John 10:39 even reports, "... they sought to arrest him, but he escaped from their hands."

Afterward, Jesus moved His ministry across the Jordan River to "... the place where John had been baptizing at first ..." (John 10:40). John 1:28 calls this place "Bethany across the Jordan." This is not the same Bethany near Jerusalem, where Mary, Martha, and Lazarus lived, but is a location with the same name, which as John wrote, lies beyond the Jordan River. While the exact location of this site is not known with complete certainty, it is believed by many to be the place referred to today as Al-Maghtas (also known as Wadi

Kharar), in the country of Jordan, and is located on the east side of the Jordan River, about six miles southeast of Jericho (UNESCO, pp. 49–50, and *The ESV Archeology Study Bible*, p. 1541). Jericho is seventeen miles east/northeast of Jerusalem (*The Eerdman's Bible Dictionary*, p. 566), so that means Al-Maghtas is about 21 miles from the Bethany where Mary, Martha, and Lazarus lived.

While He was there, a troubling situation developed for His friends back in Bethany of Judea. Lazarus became very ill. We are not told in the text of John's gospel what the illness was, but it was serious enough for them to call to Jesus for help. John writes:

> Now a certain man was sick: Lazarus of Bethany, the village of Mary and her sister Martha. And it was the Mary who anointed the Lord with ointment, and wiped His feet with her hair, whose brother Lazarus was sick. So the sisters sent *word* to Him, saying, "Lord, behold, he whom You love is sick" (John 11:1–3 NASB).

Mary and Martha knew who to contact for help in this situation. They had, no doubt, heard of and had possibly seen some of the healings that Jesus had performed up to this point in His ministry. They knew that Jesus had the power to heal and that He loved them, and so their expectation seems to have been that He would come as soon as He possibly could and heal Lazarus. Such a response from the Lord would minimize the pain and the grief. They appear to have assumed, as many do today as well, that when someone cares about you, has the power to help you, and they know you are suffering, then they are going to do everything they can to help you as quickly as possible. But in this case, as we shall see in the chapters that follow, this was not what Jesus did.

Chapter 3

Jesus' First Response

He delayed

While considering Jesus' response to Mary and Martha's cry for help, it is helpful to look at both His initial response and His complete response. First, we will consider His initial response. Remember, Mary and Martha's apparent expectation was that He would respond by coming as quickly as possible to their aid. He did not. The text says, "So when He heard that he was sick, He then stayed two days *longer* in the place where He was" (John 11:6 NASB). He delayed going to them. It was not that circumstances kept Him from going sooner, but He intentionally delayed going to them. What was more, He purposely waited until He knew that Lazarus had died before He started on the journey to Bethany.

> … He said to them, "Our friend Lazarus has fallen asleep; but I am going so that I may awaken him from sleep." The disciples then said to Him, "Lord, if he has fallen asleep, he will come out of it." Now Jesus had spoken of his death, but they thought that He was speaking about actual sleep. So Jesus then said to them plainly, "Lazarus died, and I am glad for your sakes that I was not there, so that you may believe; but let's go to him" (John 11:11–15 NASB).

Jesus and His disciples waited two days before beginning the journey. Let's consider the chronology of these events for a moment. The distance to the location where John had originally been baptizing was approximately 21 miles or so from Bethany. There is a change in elevation of more than 3,500 feet downhill as one goes down from Bethany to the Jordan River (Foster, pp. 852–3). The physical condition of the messengers, and the weather would have played a part in how long such a trip would take, but it seems reasonable to believe the messengers could have reached Jesus in about one long day. If Jesus and His disciples had left immediately, and considering that it was uphill all the way to Bethany, they could likely have reached the home of Lazarus within two more days. So, allowing one day for the messengers to get to Jesus, and two days for Him to come to Bethany, Mary and Martha were possibly expecting to see Jesus in about three days from the time they sent the message. The way the text of John, Chapter 11, flows, it seems what actually happened was something like this: the messengers are sent to Jesus; Jesus waits two days where He is; Lazarus dies; Jesus begins His journey to Bethany; when He gets to Bethany Lazarus had been dead for four days (apparently, Jesus and His disciples did not hurry on their way up to Bethany). It looks like the round trip of sending Him the message and His coming to Bethany took about seven days. In any case, it seems to Mary and Martha that He arrived about four days too late. Jesus' initial response was to delay in coming to them.

We will look at Jesus' complete response more thoroughly in the next chapter, but for now, just know that though He delayed initially, He did not fail to help His friends.

So, why did He delay?

Before we try to answer that question, let us consider what the delay does NOT mean.

What the Delay Does Not Mean

The first thing that the delay does not mean is that Jesus took their pain and their grief lightly. When Jesus did arrive, even though He knew what He was going to do in terms of raising Lazarus, He took the time to listen to Martha and then to Mary. He did not say to them, "Wait, wait, wait, no need to grieve here!" Instead, He made the effort to hear them out, and to listen with sensitivity.

Jesus' responses to Martha and to Mary are not the same. He

dealt with each of them differently, according to their individual needs. Remember from the story recorded in Luke, Chapter 10, that Martha and Mary have contrasting personalities. Martha was the first to come out to meet Jesus as He drew near to Bethany. The record of their interaction is as follows:

> So when Martha heard that Jesus was coming, she went and met him, but Mary remained seated in the house. Martha said to Jesus, "Lord, if you had been here, my brother would not have died. But even now I know that whatever you ask from God, God will give you." Jesus said to her, "Your brother will rise again." Martha said to him, "I know that he will rise again in the resurrection on the last day." Jesus said to her, "I am the resurrection and the life. Whoever believes in me, though he die, yet shall he live, and everyone who lives and believes in me shall never die. Do you believe this?" She said to him, "Yes, Lord; I believe that you are the Christ, the Son of God, who is coming into the world" (John 11:20–27).

Jesus' interaction with Martha here was tender and effective. He listened to her concern, He gave her hope, and He drew from her a statement of unwavering faith. Martha, apparently, did not expect Lazarus to be raised immediately, but in spite of his death and the Lord's seemingly untimely arrival, she maintained hope for a resurrection "on the last day," and powerfully confessed that Jesus is the Christ, the Son of God. Though Martha was, no doubt, heavily grief-stricken, she was strong. She made the effort to immediately meet Jesus as He reached the edge of town, greeted Him, and conversed with Him concerning her brother's death.

Jesus' interaction with Mary, however, was different. Mary did not come out to meet Jesus initially, but "remained seated in the house" (John 11:20); but when Jesus asked for her, she was quick to come. Jesus' interaction with her did not include the kind of dialogue He had just experienced with her sister. Mary was too devastated for that. When she reached Jesus, she fell at His feet, making the same statement that if He had been there her brother would not have died, and she wept (John 11:32). As Jesus observed Mary's brokenness, He felt deeply troubled (11:33), and wept with her (11:35). Even though He knew that He would momentarily raise Lazarus, He still wept. Seeing this woman so deeply hurt by her brother's illness and death moved Him beyond words, and He simply wept with her. John 11:35, often noted as the shortest verse in the English translation of the Bible, shows His empathy. It is a verse that stands out; as it should. Though this verse is brief, it speaks volumes. He did not take the pain she was experiencing lightly.

Another thing that the delay does not mean is the idea that the Lord arrived late. Mary and Martha may have thought this before Lazarus was raised, but they soon learned that it was not true. The Son of God never arrives late. Sometimes it may seem that way to us, at least for a time, but that is because we do not know what He knows. As always, He was walking perfectly in the will of His Father.

John 9:4 (NIV) quotes Jesus as saying, "As long as it is day, we must do the works of him who sent me. Night is coming, when no one can work," and in John 11:9 (NIV), He says, "Are there not twelve hours of daylight? Anyone who walks in the daytime will not stumble, for they see by this world's light." These statements are about opportunity and timing, and they show that Jesus operated in a manner that makes the most of them both.

Mary and Martha wanted Jesus to come on their time schedule, and understandably so. Their brother's life hung in the balance. Yet Jesus did not submit to their timetable. His only method of operation was to walk perfectly in His Father's will, including His timing.

Think about how important timing is in God's creation. The earth's rotation, its orbit around the sun, and the moon's orbit around the earth are all happening with exactly the correct timing in order to sustain biological life. If any of these processes were significantly altered, our lives could be at risk. God, the Creator, has timing figured out.

The delay also, does not mean that the Lord had somehow failed to come through and meet their need for help. He did come, and He did help. It just was not in the way they expected.

There is at least one more thing the delay does not mean, and this is something very important to understand. It does not mean that He did not love them. John makes it clear to his readers that Jesus loved Mary, Martha, and Lazarus. He writes, "Lord, the one you love is sick," and, "Now Jesus loved Martha and her sister and Lazarus" (John 11:3b NIV and 11:5).

So then, why did He delay? In the chapters that follow, let's explore this all-important question. The answers will put to death forever the lie of the ages.

✦ Chapter 4 ✦

Jesus' Complete Response

He Wanted to Do More

As we read on through the text of John, Chapter 11, we see not only the Lord's initial reaction to His friends' cry for help, but His complete reaction. After taking the time to talk to, grieve with, and comfort His friends, He asked them where they had laid their brother. Then He acted.

> So Jesus, again being deeply moved within, came to the tomb. Now it was a cave, and a stone was lying against it. Jesus said, "Remove the stone." Martha, the sister of the deceased, said to Him, "Lord, by this time there will be a stench, for he has been dead four days." Jesus said to her, "Did I not say to you that if you believe, you will see the glory of God?" So they removed the stone. And Jesus raised His eyes, and said, "Father, I thank You that You have heard Me. But I knew that You always hear Me; nevertheless, because of the people standing around I said it, so that they may believe that You sent Me." And when He had said these things, He cried out with a loud voice, "Lazarus, come out!" Out came the man who had died, bound hand and foot with wrappings, and his face was wrapped around with a cloth. Jesus said to them, "Unbind him, and let him go" (John 11:38-44 NASB).

If Jesus would have come as quickly as He could have, reached Bethany before Lazarus had died, healed Lazarus from his illness, and done all that Mary and Martha expected, it would have seemed to have been a good thing; it would have met their need, and would have brought glory to God. All this appears to be good.

However, by waiting and arriving at the time He did, after Lazarus had been dead four days, prepared for burial according to the custom of the day, and laid in a tomb, and then raising him from the dead, He did a much more powerful sign, and brought much greater glory to God. His waiting was not so He would do a smaller thing, but so that He could do a bigger thing. It was not so that He would somehow do less for them, but so that He could do more! Since Lazarus had been dead four days, wrapped in linens, and laid in the tomb, and then raised, it completely eliminates any possibility that Lazarus had not really died, but had simply passed out. The ancient Jewish people believed that after three days of lying as a corpse, death was certain and the body would begin to decay (*The ESV Archeology Study Bible, p. 1567*). It was obvious to all present that only God, the Author of Life, could do such a thing. Their need was still met, and yet it brought more glory to God. He delayed, in order to do more.

So ...

To consider the next point as to what the delay does mean, it is necessary to go back to the beginning of John, Chapter 11. Here, we read a very unusual thing. It is found in Verses 5 and 6:

> Now Jesus loved Martha and her sister and Lazarus. So, when he heard that Lazarus was ill, he stayed two days longer in the place where he was.

What is interesting about these verses is that they do not say something like, "Now Jesus loved Martha, Mary, and Lazarus; *nevertheless,* He stayed two days longer in the place where He was." Rather, it clearly says, "So." The word translated "so" here in the English Standard Version is the Greek word *oun,* (White, p. 374) which is a *"particle expressing sequence or consequence"* (Vine, p. 124). It is the same word used in verse 3, which says, "So the sisters sent to Him, saying ..." The reason the sisters sent to Him is due to the previously-mentioned fact that their brother was ill. The idea mentioned beforehand has a cause and effect relationship with the idea mentioned afterward. This is "so," therefore, that happened. In fact, the Greek word *oun* is often translated as *therefore* in English versions of the Bible. Most modern English translations of the New Testament render the word in this verse as "so," while some use "therefore." In other words, it appears that His love for Martha, Mary, and Lazarus was His motivation for waiting. He did not just wait despite loving them, He waited **because** He loved them. He wanted something greater for them than immediate deliverance from their pain and grief.

In this instance we see that love does not always chose the easiest path, or the path with the least pain or the least grief, but it always chooses the best path. God saw something in this incident that caused Him to conclude that the best path for this family was to allow them to temporarily experience an actual increase in grief. Mary and Martha went from having a brother who was sick, to having a brother who was dead. According to Verse 6, Jesus took this path because of His love for Martha, Mary, and Lazarus. He saw that the good result that would come far outweighed a temporary increase in grief.

❦   Chapter 5   ❧

For the Glory of God

Now we must look at what is probably the most central reason as to why Jesus delayed in going to assist His friends Mary, Martha, and Lazarus. He states the reason Himself in John 11:4.

> So the sisters sent to him, saying, "Lord, he whom you love is ill." But when Jesus heard it he said, "This illness does not lead to death. It is for the glory of God, so that the Son of God may be glorified through it" (John 11:3–4).

It was for the glory of God. Jesus knew the outcome in advance. That is why, even though Lazarus dies before He reaches him, He states, "This illness does not lead to death." He knew that He would raise Lazarus, and that the event of raising him would bring more glory to God than would a quick healing.

If you spend time with Christian people, you will soon hear comments about glorifying God, and that's as it should be, but I wonder if we have carefully thought through what this actually means. Let us take the time here to search out this concept a little more. I believe that doing so will itself glorify God.

God is Not Selfish

As I was reading about all of this in my Bible, a thought popped into my head. Maybe this thought has popped into your head at some point, too, and maybe not, but I think that it has occurred to many people. The idea is this, "*Did God let Mary, Martha, and Lazarus wade deeper into trouble and grief in order to get something out of this for Himself? Does He seek His own glory at their expense?"* As the Apostle Paul has said in many of his letters, "May it never be!" Would the Lord ever do anything for His own benefit at the expense of His people? Certainly not!

This idea is just another version of the lie of the ages. It is nothing more than a repeat of the notion that we suffer pain and grief because God does not really have our best interests at heart. The idea that God would do anything for His own benefit at the cost of any other person is completely false. That is not how He operates. It is not within His nature to function in that manner. Rather, He always seeks the benefit of His people, even at His own cost. Consider the following verse:

> For God so loved the world, that he gave his only Son, that whoever believes in him should not perish but have eternal life (John 3:16).

Here we see God pouring Himself out and giving up His beloved Son so that others may live.

Or how about these passages:

> "For even the Son of Man came not to be served but to serve, and to give his life as a ransom for many" (Mark 10:45).

> The thief comes only to steal and kill and destroy. I came that they may have life and have it abundantly. I am the good shepherd. The good shepherd lays down his life for the sheep (John 10:10–11).

Here we see Jesus contrasting Himself with a selfish thief. The thief is of a nature that seeks gain for himself at the expense of others. He is willing to destroy and kill others, if necessary, to get what he wants. It is not so with the good shepherd. He is not self-oriented. Rather, He lays down His own life to save the sheep.

Here is the nature of God on display:

> For while we were still weak, at the right time Christ died for the ungodly. For one will scarcely die for a righteous

person—though perhaps for a good person one would dare even to die—but God shows his love for us in that while we were still sinners, Christ died for us (Romans 5:6–8).

The Father and the Son are of one nature, and that nature is not self-oriented.

Here is what we know from what we have studied thus far. Jesus loved Mary, Martha, and Lazarus. When Lazarus became ill, they sent for Him, but He did not come right away. He delayed long enough so that Lazarus died. The text of John's gospel states that He did this because He loved them, and because it was for the glory of God. It brought more glory to God for Jesus to raise Lazarus from the dead than it would have for Him to quickly heal him. God is not selfish, and therefore, never seeks something for Himself at our expense. So, we can only conclude that if these events were going to bring more glory to God, then to do so somehow brought a significant benefit to Mary, Martha, and Lazarus! We saw that the Lord did not take their pain or their grief at all lightly, and so He would not take them down this path unless there was a very good reason. It had to be worth it. It had to be for their benefit in the end. Now we must explore how it benefited them for God to be glorified in this way.

To Glorify God is to Relate to Him Properly

The Scriptures teach that glory belongs to the Lord, and that it is, therefore, right for Him to be glorified (*e.g.*1 Peter 4:11), but what does it mean to glorify God? Let's take a look at some definitions.

The word translated *glory* in John 11:4 is the Greek word *doxa*, and the word *glorify* is *doxazo*, which is simply the verb form of the same word (White, p. 374, and Vine, pp. 152–153). Berry defines *doxa* as follows:

1) favorable recognition or estimation, honor, renown

2) the appearance, the manifestation of that which calls forth praise; … (Berry, p. 42)

Vine says *doxa*, as it applies to God, is the "acknowledgment of the exhibition of His attributes and ways" (Vine, p. 153). Of *doxazo* he says, it is "to magnify, extol, praise ... especially of glorifying God, i.e., ascribing honor to Him, acknowledging Him as to His being, attributes, and acts ..." (Vine, p. 152).

It appears, therefore, that to give glory to God basically means to recognize Him for who He is; He is good, and He, therefore, does good things. To glorify Him is to recognize His nature and attributes, and to celebrate them, especially with others. It is to give Him proper credit for His good and powerful works. It is to give Him honor. It is to perceive Him and talk about Him in a positive light. This would necessarily include trusting Him, having faith in Him, honoring Him, relying on Him, submitting to Him, and loving Him. When we glorify God, we are recognizing His attributes and acts for what they are, and therefore, it is a result of perceiving Him accurately and relating to Him properly.

It is now evident that when people believe the lie of the ages mentioned earlier, that this is the opposite of glorifying God. The lie of the ages says that the reason we suffer is because God does not have our best interests at heart. It is to doubt His good intentions, and to consider Him to be untrustworthy. It is to believe that He doesn't care, that He is not interested in what is going on in one's life, or that He isn't powerful enough to help. Taking this stance leads one to doubt God's goodness and often results in anger towards Him. For some, it may lead to an actual casting off of submission and obedience, resulting in open rebellion against Him.

Perceiving the Lord in a positive light and confessing so to others is the opposite of grumbling and complaining. It is now rather easy to see why the Scriptures teach God's people not to embrace an attitude of complaining.

In the Old Testament, when the Israelites were wandering in the wilderness after the exodus, they sometimes experienced a lack of comfort. Some were tempted to doubt God's intentions and they began to complain. This usually brought rather disastrous results for them.

In the New Covenant, we are taught to give thanks in all

circumstances, and to do all things without grumbling or disputing (1 Thessalonians 5:18; Philippians 2:14–15). Doing so protects us from the catastrophic results of believing the lie of the ages. When God's people complain about their circumstances or about His provision, it not only fails to honor Him properly, but it can discourage those around us who hear it. We may not feel very good about pain and grief when they come, but we can still trust God's intentions, and know that He always has our best interests at heart.

Mary and Martha did not believe the lie of the ages. Even though they were hurting and did not understand at first why the Lord had delayed in coming to them, they remained responsive to Him and continued to believe in who He was. They continued to trust God in the face of difficult circumstances and were not disappointed for having done so.

Glorifying God is about relating to Him properly. When we view God in a positive light, with full trust in His good nature and good intentions, then we are relating to Him in agreement with who He really is, and with the honor due to Him. When a human being glorifies God, then the creation is functioning as He intended. God's Word teaches us that He is love, and that He loves each human person fully and completely (John 3:16; 1 John 4; Romans 5; and many other verses). He desires to have a rich and intimate fellowship with each one of us. When this occurs, it is a mutually beneficial thing for both God and the other person involved. God is pleased, and the human person is richly blessed. It is not about God seeking to please Himself, it is about His including each one of us in a process in which we are going to be richly blessed, as well.

On the night in which Jesus was betrayed and subsequently arrested, He spent some time praying with and praying for His disciples. John, Chapter 17, records one of these prayers. There we are given a glimpse from the heart of God, concerning His intention for both creating and redeeming mankind. Here are some excerpts:

> Jesus spoke these things; and raising His eyes to heaven, He said, "Father, the hour has come; glorify Your Son, so that the Son may glorify You, just as You gave Him authority over all mankind, so that to all whom You have given Him,

He may give eternal life. And this is eternal life, that they may know You, the only true God, and Jesus Christ whom You have sent. I glorified You on the earth by accomplishing the work which You have given Me to do. And now You, Father, glorify Me together with Yourself, with the glory which I had with You before the world existed" (John 17:1–5 NASB).

"I am not asking on behalf of these alone, but also for those who believe in Me through their word, that they may all be one; just as You, Father, *are* in Me and I in You, that they also may be in Us, so that the world may believe that You sent Me. The glory which You have given Me I also have given to them, so that they may be one, just as We are one; I in them and You in Me, that they may be perfected in unity, so that the world may know that You sent Me, and You loved them, just as You loved Me. Father, I desire that they also, whom You have given Me, be with Me where I am, so that they may see My glory which You have given Me, for You loved Me before the foundation of the world" (John 17:20–24 NASB).

In the prayer above Jesus revealed that He had completed the Father's work in order to glorify Him. He asked the Father to glorify the Son. He revealed that sharing in glory was experienced between the Father and the Son before the world ever existed. He stated that He had given to His disciples the glory which the Father had given Him, and that this glory is directly tied to experiencing oneness with the Father and the Son. It is tied to rich and intimate fellowship with Them.

Glorifying God is central in purpose for God's people. If asked today what the central and eternal purpose for the Church of the Lord Jesus Christ is, many people would say things like "make disciples, reach the lost, proclaim the gospel, and teach God's Word." In other words, the Church exists for evangelism and discipleship. Yet, even though evangelism and discipleship are central activities for the Church at this present time, it will not always be so. Once the present heavens and earth have passed away, and God's people are rejoicing with the Lord in His eternal kingdom, there will no longer be the need for these activities to happen in the same way. Glorifying God, however, is an eternal activity of the Lord's Church. Consider the Apostle Paul's statement to the Ephesians:

> Now to him who is able to do far more abundantly than all that we ask or think, according to the power at work within us, to him be glory in the church and in Christ Jesus throughout all generations, forever and ever. Amen (Ephesians 3:20–21).

This verse states that glorifying God is something that is central in the activity of His Church both now and forevermore. Although evangelism and discipleship are extremely important missions for the Church right now, they are nevertheless temporal activities, whereas glorifying God is an eternal activity for the Church.

The central point here is that glorifying God is not just some religious cliché. It is central to the purpose of the Lord's Church. It is directly tied to relating to God properly in oneness and in intimacy. It is to view Him in agreement with the reality of who He is; it is to respond to Him in agreement with the reality of who He is; it is to act in a manner that is in agreement with the reality of who He is. Glorifying God is directly tied to relating to Him in an intimate way, in which we share in a rich fellowship and oneness with Him. I believe it is evident that one reason God created humans in the first place was to share with them in a rich and intimate fellowship. He redeemed humans to restore this rich and intimate fellowship after it had been broken by sin.

The Lord wanted to draw Mary, Martha, and Lazarus deeper into this experience. The raising of Lazarus accomplished that more than the quick healing of Lazarus would have done. Jesus' delay in coming to them was for their benefit.

Chapter 6

The Results from Raising Lazarus

Mary, Martha, and Lazarus Glorified God

There is no doubt that after Jesus raised Lazarus from the dead that Mary, Martha, and Lazarus were grateful to Him for what He did. They were surely drawn closer to the Lord. Their actions following the event show this to be true.

John, Chapter 12, describes events that took place not long after the raising of Lazarus.

> Six days before the Passover, Jesus therefore came to Bethany, where Lazarus was, whom Jesus had raised from the dead. So they gave a dinner for him there. Martha served, and Lazarus was one of those reclining with him at table. Mary therefore took a pound of expensive ointment made from pure nard, and anointed the feet of Jesus and wiped his feet with her hair. The house was filled with the fragrance of the perfume (John 12:1-3).

There is evidence that this event was tied directly to the raising of Lazarus. Notice how John wants the reader to make note that Lazarus was present and mentions him as being the one "whom Jesus had raised from the dead" (vs. 1). Also, at the beginning of Chapter 11, when John is preparing to describe the events surrounding the raising of Lazarus, he is careful to introduce Mary as being the one who "anointed the Lord with ointment and wiped his feet with her hair" (John 11:2). It seems that John wants to make clear the point that these two events are related—the raising of Lazarus and the anointing by Mary.

Matthew and Mark also mention this event in their gospels. Some may think that Matthew and Mark's accounts refer to a different event, since they both record it in sequence after Jesus' triumphal entry into Jerusalem. Yet the similarities outweigh any differences in the accounts. All accounts have a woman anointing Jesus with a very expensive ointment. All describe the disciples (John names Judas) as complaining about the use of the expensive ointment. All mention Jesus as commenting that they would always have the poor among them, but that they would not always have Him. All have Jesus mentioning His own burial. The best explanation seems to be that all three are describing the same event (Foster, pp. 1079–1081). Matthew and Mark choose not to mention the woman's name, but John tells us that it was Mary of Bethany, Lazarus' sister. Matthew and Mark relate the story after telling us of the triumphal entry and other events that took place during the final week of Jesus' earthly ministry, but they do not say specifically when it happened. They may place it where they do because of thematic reasons, rather than chronological ones. It comes right between mentioning the plot to kill Jesus, and the record of Judas going to the chief priests to betray Him. Both have to do with Jesus' death, as does the anointing, since it is said to be for His burial. John, on the other hand, appears to be more concerned with the chronology of the event.

> Six days before the Passover, Jesus therefore came to Bethany, where Lazarus was, whom he had raised from the dead. So they gave a dinner for him there. Martha served, and Lazarus was one of those reclining with him at table.
>
> (John 12:1–2)

If we put the accounts together as one, the following scenario is possible: Jesus came to Bethany six days before the Passover. After He arrived, some of His friends wanted to have a dinner for Him. Simon, the Leper, offered to have the event at his place, probably because Jesus had previously healed him of his leprosy, and he now wanted to honor Jesus (he could not still be a leper and be living in his house and having people over for dinner). Martha must have said, "I'll bring the food and serve." Lazarus was there, reclining at the table with Jesus and His disciples. Mary came in and anointed His head (Matthew and Mark) and His feet (John) with the expensive ointment made of pure nard. Judas then complained about the use of the expensive nard as being extravagant, and Jesus gave His response.

The point to be made here is that these friends of Jesus wanted to honor Him. They had each experienced some form of help or deliverance from Him, having walked through a significant difficulty while experiencing both the Lord's comfort and His healing, and they now wanted to honor Him, and thus glorify God. This is especially so with Mary. Judas estimated the value of the ointment to be about 300 denarii (John 12:5).

Today, when we hear 300 denarii, it might not mean much to us, unless we are familiar with first century units of measurement. It is not very difficult, however, to pinpoint what this is worth. In a parable about laborers contracted to work in the vineyard of a master and landowner, recorded in Matthew, Chapter 20, the workers originally agreed to work for one day in the vineyard for a denarius. So, a denarius was a day's wage for a common laborer. If the ointment was worth 300 denarii, that equates to 300 days' wages. If you remove the sabbaths and holy feasts as nonworking days, that is at least one year's wages! Why would Mary be willing to spend a year's wages on using ointment to honor the Lord? Because she had been through a trying situation, she had called on the Lord for help, and the Lord delivered her (as well as Martha and Lazarus). She spared no expense to honor Him. We are now seeing a fulfillment of Jesus' words that the sickness of Lazarus was not for death, but so that God would be glorified.

> ... and call upon me in the day of trouble;
> I will deliver you, and you shall glorify me (Psalm 50:15).

Mary, Martha, and Lazarus glorified God.

More People Believed in Jesus

Once Lazarus had died, several people came to comfort Mary and Martha. It stands to reason that more people would come to comfort them due to their brother's death than would have come to visit due to his being ill.

Among those who came for this purpose were a number from among a group that John, Chapter 11 describes as "the Jews." They were there when Mary went out to meet Jesus at the edge of town (vs. 31) and were therefore present when Jesus wept with Mary (vs. 36). They were there when Jesus raised Lazarus from the dead. John reports that due to seeing the raising of Lazarus, many of those from among the Jews began believing in Jesus (vs. 45). These were some of the same people who had engaged in heated debates with Jesus, as recorded in John, Chapters 2, 5, 7, 8, and 10. This term obviously refers to the leaders of the Jewish people, because it is used for the group that debated with Jesus at these various times, and for the group that debated with the blind man who had been healed in John, Chapter 9. They had the authority to excommunicate people from temple access, and so the people are described as fearing them (John 9:22). John says that it was many from among this group, "the Jews," that began to believe in Jesus after witnessing the raising of Lazarus.

Jesus' Entry into Jerusalem Was Impacted

On the first day of the final week of Jesus' earthly ministry, Jesus fulfilled prophesy by riding triumphantly into Jerusalem on a donkey's colt. This event is mentioned by all four gospels, thus highlighting its importance. But it is John who records the impact that the raising of Lazarus had on this monumental event. Here is John's account:

> The next day the large crowd that had come to the feast heard that Jesus was coming to Jerusalem. So they took branches of palm trees and went out to meet him, crying out, "Hosanna! Blessed is he who comes in the name of the Lord, even the King of Israel!" And Jesus found a young donkey and sat on it, just as it is written, "Fear not, daughter of Zion; behold, your king is coming, sitting on a donkey's colt!"

His disciples did not understand these things at first, but when Jesus was glorified, then they remembered that these things had been written about him and had been done to him. **The crowd that had been with him when he called Lazarus out of the tomb and raised him from the dead continued to bear witness. The reason why the crowd went to meet him was that they heard he had done this sign** (John 12:12–18—emphasis added).

John states in the verses above that the size, interest, and enthusiasm of this crowd at the triumphal entry was impacted by what they were hearing about Jesus having raised Lazarus from the dead.

The Religious Leaders Reacted

There is no question as to the fact that the raising of Lazarus stirred up the Pharisees (religious leaders) and the chief priests of the Jews. When they saw that many of their own number were beginning to believe in Jesus, they became highly alarmed. John writes:

Many of the Jews therefore, who had come with Mary and had seen what he [Jesus] did, believed in him, but some of them went to the Pharisees and told them what Jesus had done. So the chief priests and the Pharisees gathered the council and said, "What are we to do? For this man performs many signs. If we let him go on like this, everyone will believe in him, and the Romans will come and take away both our place and our nation" (John 11:45–48).

And,

So from that day on they made plans to put him to death.
(John 11:53)

It is really very sad that they had allowed themselves to get into this state—a state in which it was more important for them to do what they thought was expedient to protect their positions, than to believe in someone who was helping people, healing people, and even raising people from the dead. Obviously, God had to be working through this man, yet their best reaction was to attempt to figure out a way to stop Him, and to stop the people from believing in Him, even if it meant plotting to murder an innocent man.

So, they put the word out, as the Passover drew near, that if anyone saw Jesus, it should be reported to them immediately, so that they could have Him arrested (John 11:57).

As the Passover was about to start, more and more interest developed in what had happened to Lazarus.

> When the large crowd of the Jews learned that Jesus was there, they came, not only on account of him but also to see Lazarus, whom he had raised from the dead. So the chief priests made plans to put Lazarus to death as well, because on account of him many of the Jews were going away and believing in Jesus (John 12:9–11).

The Jewish leaders were driven to such insane levels of jealousy that at this point they were plotting to kill Lazarus, as well as Jesus! God was performing miracles in their midst, and they were literally working to undo these same miracles.

Then the triumphal entry of Jesus into Jerusalem occurred.

> So the Pharisees said to one another, "You see that you are gaining nothing. Look, the world has gone after him" (John 12:19).

This intensified effort on the part of the Pharisees and the chief priests eventually led to their success in arresting Jesus (through His betrayal by Judas), and having Him put to death. The death of Jesus and His subsequent resurrection were central elements in God's plan to complete redemption on behalf of all humanity.

Summary of the Results

So, let us quickly summarize. When Lazarus became very ill,

Jesus could have rushed to his side and immediately healed him from the illness, but instead, He delayed. He allowed Lazarus to die, causing Mary and Martha to move deeper into pain and grief. When He arrived, He comforted them both, and then raised Lazarus from the dead. The results of having raised Lazarus, rather than quickly healing him, were that Mary, Martha, and Lazarus glorified God more than they would otherwise have done. They came to know Jesus more deeply as the One with power over life and death, and so they (together with other friends) hosted a dinner to honor Him. Mary came in and anointed Jesus with a perfume that was worth a year's wages. Many other people began to believe in Jesus; even some of the Jewish leaders did this. A large crowd gathered for the Passover, and many of them heard of what Jesus had done for Lazarus. The triumphal entry then occurred. The chief priests and the Pharisees intensified their efforts to arrest and kill Jesus. They finally succeeded, and through Jesus' death and resurrection, atonement for the sins of the world was accomplished.

All of this, of course, took place according to the predetermined plan and foreknowledge of God (Acts 2:23). Yet it is interesting to note that God loved Mary, Martha, and Lazarus enough to include them in such a special way in the events leading up to His salvation plan of the ages. Why did Jesus delay in coming to them? Because He loved them enough to give them a significant role in glorifying God in this huge manner.

When we glorify God, we are blessed, and He is pleased. When the Lord draws us deeper into situations that will result in more glory for Him, it is because He loves us; desires to reveal more of Himself to us; and wants to enhance our relationship with Him. This may involve pain, but the pain is temporary, and the positive result is permanent and is more than worth it.

Chapter 7

A Foundation for Good Relationships

Relating to One Another

One does not have to read very far in the Scriptures to see that God is relationship oriented. The greatest commandment of all, according to Jesus, is to love God with all of one's heart, soul, mind, and strength (Mark 12:30); and the second greatest commandment is to love one's neighbor as oneself (Mark 12:31). Both commandments are relationship oriented.

To understand these commandments better, it is important to understand how love behaves and how it is measured. Jesus talked as though love can vary in degree and can be measured as to its greatness. He made statements about the greatness of love. Consider John 3:16 for example, "For God so loved the world, that he gave his only Son, that whoever believes in him should not perish but have eternal life." How much did God love the world? This much, He gave. How much was He willing to give? He gave His only Son. In this verse, the amount that God loved is measured by what He was willing to give, at His own cost, for the world's benefit.

Here is another example, "Greater love has no one than this, that someone lay down his life for his friends" (John 15:13). How is the greatness of love measured in this statement? In the same way that we have just seen in the previous verse, by how much one is willing to give or sacrifice to benefit another. One cannot give more than one's own life, so Jesus describes this as the greatest love.

Relationships work best when there is love operating between the parties involved. This is true of friendships, marriages, partnerships, dealings with relatives, neighbors, and coworkers. When each person is focused on the other person's needs, rather than their own, then the relationship will thrive. Once they turn toward themselves and focus on their own needs first, then the relationship will begin to break down. Hear the Apostle Paul on this:

> Do nothing from selfish ambition or conceit, but in humility count others more significant than yourselves. Let each of you look not only to his own interests, but also to the interests of others (Philippians 2:3–4).

The New Testament Scriptures are full of exhortations for God's people to do things for one another. Love one another; outdo one another in showing honor; welcome one another; instruct one another; greet one another; care for one another; comfort one another; serve one another; bear one another's burdens; forgive one another; submit to one another; admonish one another; encourage one another; and build one another up are just some of the exhortations found in the letters of the Apostles.

Human relationships work best when each person is focused on meeting the needs of the other person, and they begin to fall apart when either party starts to focus on having their own needs met first.

Dr. Emerson Eggerichs has written a book for married couples entitled *Love and Respect*. In this book, he points out a dynamic in marriage that he describes as the Energizing Cycle. The concept, based on Ephesians 5:33 (Eggerichs, p. 14), states that his love motivates her respect, and her respect motivates his love (Eggerichs, pp. 115–116). When the husband interacts in ways that the wife perceives as loving, she is more motivated to treat him with respect, and when the wife treats her husband in a manner that he perceives as respectful, he is more motivated to react to her with love. In this way, a husband and wife can build a cycle of behavior in which they increasingly motivate and energize one another. In his book, Dr. Eggerichs provides husbands and wives with many ideas for keeping the Energizing Cycle going.

Romantic love works this way, in general. The more you esteem, respect, and value another, the more important it is when that person returns this esteem, respect, and value to you.

Relating to God

I believe this basic concept of putting the interest of others before our own is true of our relationship with God, as well. The relationship works properly when each party makes the other person and their desires the focus of the attention, and not our own desires. When this is working right, God is focused on blessing us, while we are focused on praising and glorifying Him. Of course, God already has the correct focus for this to happen. We are the objects of His love. Everything He does regarding us is born of His nature, and His nature includes love for us.

We, on the other hand, are not always properly focused. So, it is often necessary for the Lord to take action to move us into the proper frame of mind; and sometimes, this involves permitting suffering in our lives.

There is no question that the Lord calls His followers to a selfless mindset. Consider these statements from Jesus:

"Whoever seeks to preserve his life will lose it, but whoever loses his life will keep it" (Luke 17:33).

And he said to all, "If anyone would come after me, let him deny himself and take up his cross daily and follow me. For whoever would save his life will lose it, but whoever loses his life for my sake will save it" (Luke 9:23–24).

The more we make loving God and seeking to please Him our primary focus, the more we are blessed, as well. God relates to us in a completely selfless manner. When we relate to Him in this way, the relationship blossoms and grows, and functions the way He intends.

Some people only think of the Lord when they are facing a problem that stretches them beyond their own ability to solve. When things are going well, God is the last One on their mind. Their focus is on pleasing themselves, with no regard to what His Word has to say. Then, suddenly, trouble hits and they are looking for His help. Of course, it is not wrong for anyone to seek God's help when they have trouble. In Chapter 9, we will be looking at the fact that He instructs us to do this. It is wrong, however, if that is the only time someone looks to Him.

Imagine if you treated anyone else you know in this way. You never call, visit, or spend time with them. You fail to respond to their invitations, messages, or social media posts. Then, when you have a debt or a bill you cannot pay, you are suddenly contacting them and asking for help. I do not think the friendship would be very healthy.

Like any relationship, our relationship with the Lord functions best when one's focus is not on oneself. Jesus taught that the greatest commandment of all is to love God with all of one's heart, soul, mind, and strength (Mark 12:30). If we do not love Him in this way, it is we who are broken, not Him.

☙ Chapter 8 ❧

Destroying the Lie of the Ages

God Understands Suffering

When we suffer, we can be tempted to become angry with God. We may begin to think, *He does not know what it is like to suffer. He is in heaven where everything is good.* This idea is an offshoot of the lie of the ages. implying that God does not know what we are going through, or that He does not care. Nothing, however, could be further from the truth.

The writer of the New Testament book entitled Hebrews makes plain that God understands suffering very well, from the inside out. Look at what he has to say in his letter:

> … we see him who for a little while was made lower than the angels, namely Jesus, crowned with glory and honor because of the suffering of death, so that by the grace of God he might taste death for everyone.
> For it was fitting that he, for whom and by whom all things exist, in bringing many sons to glory, should make the founder of their salvation perfect through suffering (Hebrews 2:9–10).

And,

> In the days of his flesh, Jesus offered up prayers and supplications, with loud cries and tears, to him who was able to save him from death, and he was heard because of his reverence. Although he was a son, he learned obedience through what he suffered. And being made perfect, he became the source of eternal salvation to all who obey him,

being designated by God a high priest after the order of Melchizedek (Hebrews 5:7–10).

These words are nothing short of astounding! Here we see that the eternal Son of God is said to have been made perfect and to have learned obedience through suffering. How can this be? In Jesus dwells the fullness of deity in bodily form (Colossians 2:9). He is holy, innocent, and unstained (Hebrews 7:26), and yet it is said of Him that He was made perfect and learned obedience through suffering. We must think about that. The Son of God being the eternal Word made flesh and sinless, is said to have been made perfect through suffering.

We must remember that even though the Son has always been the eternal Word, He has not always been a man. There is a point in time when the "Word became flesh and dwelt among us" (John 1:14). The writer of Hebrews quotes Psalm 2 and Psalm 110 with the following statement:

> So also Christ did not exalt himself to be made a high priest, but was appointed by him who said to him, "You are my Son, today I have begotten you"; as he says also in another place, "You are a priest forever, after the order of Melchizedek" (Hebrews 5:5–6).

So, there was some point when these statements were made by the Father to the Son. The Son has always been the eternal Word, but He had to partake of flesh and blood (Hebrews 2:14); "he had to be made like his brothers in every respect ..." (Hebrews 2:17). In other words, He had to become a flesh and blood mortal man.

An interesting fact concerning the statement from Psalm 2:7, "... You are my Son; today I have begotten you" is that it is also quoted by the Apostle Paul as recorded in the book of Acts, Chapter 13. Paul and Barnabas were visiting the synagogue in Antioch of the region of Pisidia and were invited to share a word of encouragement with those present that day. Paul took the opportunity as an occasion to share the good news about Jesus, and in so doing he quotes this verse from Psalm 2. What is interesting is that he did not apply the verse to Jesus' conception or birth, as some might think he would do, but instead, applied it to His resurrection. So, according to Paul, this statement made by the Father to the Son is made at the resurrection. That is to say, the Son of God, Jesus, was made to partake of flesh and blood, to become a mortal man, and to experience everything we humanly experience in terms of temptation, discomfort, pain, suffering, and death. He overcame them all, and **then** He sat down at the right hand of Majesty on high and took His seat as the Great High Priest, according to the order of Melchizedek. Jesus, the Son of Man and the Son of God, has been given all authority in heaven and on earth (Matthew 28); He has been made the Great High Priest, and the Judge of all, but He did not (as a human) take His seat as such until He had experienced temptation, pain, suffering, and even death. He now understands these things from the inside out. I believe that is what the writer of Hebrews means when he says that the Son was made perfect through what He suffered. He knows what it is like to live in a poor family; to be hungry; to be thirsty; to be tired; to be insulted; to be rejected; to have a loved one die; to have to work hard; to sweat; to be falsely accused; to be publicly humiliated; to be unjustly punished; to be tortured; and to have your loved ones see you go through it all.

Read this again:

Therefore he had to be made like his brothers in every respect, so that he might become a merciful and faithful high priest in the service of God, to make propitiation for the sins of the people. For because he himself has suffered when tempted, he is able to help those who are being tempted (Hebrews 2:17–18).

Since then we have a great high priest who has passed through the heavens, Jesus, the Son of God, let us hold fast our confession. For we do not have a high priest who is unable to sympathize with our weaknesses, but one who in every respect has been tempted as we are, yet without sin. Let us then with confidence draw near to the throne of grace, that we may receive mercy and find grace to help in time of need (Hebrews 4:14–16).

He understands from the inside out everything that each one of us faces in terms of pain, trouble, grief, and temptation. No one can stand before Him and claim, "But You just do not know what it is like to suffer what I have suffered." By what He has suffered, He has demonstrated that He understands, and that He cares. He has completely destroyed the lie of the ages.

Chapter 9

God Uses Suffering to Benefit His People

The Lord is a Refiner of Silver and of Gold

As we have just seen, the Lord thoroughly understands suffering. We have also seen that He is unselfish, and that His actions toward His people are always born of His love for us. So, we can reasonably conclude that when He does permit suffering in our lives that He has a good reason for doing so. One of the reasons taught in the Scriptures for the Lord allowing His people to experience affliction is to purify them. There is no doubt that when people experience pain and suffering, these can have a purifying effect in their lives. The Scriptures teach that God sometimes uses pain to purify people, like one who is a refiner of silver and of gold.

> For you, O God, have tested us;
>   you have tried us as silver is tried.
> You brought us into the net;
>   you laid a crushing burden on our backs;
> you let men ride over our heads;
>   we went through fire and through water;
> yet you have brought us out to a place of abundance.
> Psalm 66:10–12

But who can endure the day of his coming, and who can stand when he appears? For he is like a refiner's fire and like fullers' soap. He will sit as a refiner and purifier of silver, and he will purify the sons of Levi and refine them like gold and silver, and they will bring offerings in righteousness to the LORD (Malachi 3:2–3).

"And I will put this third into the fire,
  and refine them as one refines silver,
  and test them as gold is tested.
They will call upon my name,
  and I will answer them.
I will say, 'They are my people';
  and they will say, 'The LORD is my God.'"

Zechariah 13:9

Therefore thus says the LORD of hosts: "Behold, I will refine them and test them, for what else can I do, because of my people?" (Jeremiah 9:7).

In ancient times, refinement was accomplished by means of placing the precious metal in a crucible, sometimes using other metals such as lead as a flux, and then applying enough heat so as to remove the impurities (Harrison, p. 84 and p. 91). The heat for refining is used as a symbol in these passages for the suffering that people went through. The suffering is intended to remove impurities from the heart just as impurities are removed from precious metal by heat. God is portrayed as being like a goldsmith. He starts with something that has value, but it needs refinement, and so He works it through a process designed to remove impurities. The goldsmith is left with a pure and more valuable product.

If, when we are afflicted, we run to God, He will comfort; He will eventually heal us; and He will skim the impurities from our lives; but if, when we are afflicted, we begin to believe the lie of the ages, and turn away from God, we can end up hardening, with the impurities still in place.

God wants to purify us like a goldsmith working to refine and to purify the gold. Then He will have an item that can serve a much greater purpose than it ever could if it were to remain impure.

The Lord Uses Suffering to Provoke Repentance

There are times when the suffering we experience is brought about by foolish choices we make. Not all suffering is the result of having made bad choices, but it is wrong to think that none of it is. The Scriptures clearly teach that the Lord sometimes disciplines His people when they make sinful or foolish choices. His intention in this is to provoke repentance, or to bring about a change in heart in the person or group of persons with whom He is dealing.

> For consider Him who has endured such hostility by sinners against Himself, so that you will not grow weary and lose heart. You have not yet resisted to the point of shedding blood in your striving against sin; and you have forgotten the exhortation which is addressed to you as sons.
>
> "MY SON, DO NOT REGARD LIGHTLY THE DISCIPLINE OF THE LORD,
> NOR FAINT WHEN YOU ARE PUNISHED BY HIM;
> FOR WHOM THE LORD LOVES HE DISCIPLINES,
> AND HE PUNISHES EVERY SON WHOM HE ACCEPTS."
>
> It is for discipline that you endure; God deals with you as with sons; for what son is there whom *his* father does not discipline? But if you are without discipline, of which all have become partakers, then you are illegitimate children and not sons. Furthermore, we had earthly fathers to discipline us, and we respected *them*; shall we not much more be subject to the Father of spirits and live? For they disciplined *us* for a short time as seemed best to them, but He *disciplines us* for *our* good, so that we may share His holiness. For the moment, all discipline seems not to be pleasant, but painful; yet to those who have been trained by it, afterward it yields the peaceful fruit of righteousness (Hebrews 12:3–11 NASB).
>
> Those whom I love, I reprove and discipline, so be zealous and repent (Revelation 3:19).

Consider the case of the nations of Israel and Judah in the time leading up to their captivity and exile. During the eighth century BC, God's people, the northern kingdom of Israel, were conquered by the Assyrians, and late in the seventh century BC, His people in the southern kingdom of Judah were conquered and taken captive by the Babylonians. Why did these events happen? They happened because God's people had repeatedly made foolish and sinful choices. The Lord had stated in the laws of Israel that if they obeyed Him, He would bless them, and that if they disobeyed Him and worshiped idols, then they would be punished.

> When you father children and children's children, and have grown old in the land, if you act corruptly by making a carved image in the form of anything, and by doing what is evil in the sight of the LORD your God, so as to provoke Him to anger, I call heaven and earth to witness against you today, that you will soon utterly perish from the land that you are going over the Jordan to possess. You will not live long in it, but will be utterly destroyed. And the LORD will scatter you among the peoples, and you will be left few in number among the nations where the LORD will drive you (Deuteronomy 4:25–27).

This statement was repeatedly ignored by the Israelites. He sent warning after warning. The majority of the content recorded in the major and minor prophets of the Old Testament contains warnings for God's people (and in some cases, the nations around them, as well) that if they did not stop sinning and serving false gods, then they would be punished. Ezekiel, for example, proclaims:

> And the word of the LORD came to me: "Son of man, the house of Israel has become dross to me; all of them are bronze and tin and iron and lead in the furnace; they are dross of silver. Therefore thus says the Lord GOD: Because you have all become dross, therefore, behold, I will gather you into the midst of Jerusalem. As one gathers silver and bronze and iron and lead and tin into a furnace, to blow the fire on it in order to melt it, so I will gather you in my anger and in my wrath, and I will put you in and melt you. I will gather you and blow on you with the fire of my wrath, and you shall be melted in the midst of it. As silver is melted in a furnace, so you shall be melted in the midst of it, and you shall know that I am the LORD; I have poured out my wrath upon you" (Ezekiel 22:17–22).

Yet even though the Lord expressed His anger with the children of Israel in this way, and brought punishment upon them, it is evident in the passage above that His intention is not to destroy His people altogether, but to purify them of their dross. The imagery of refining precious metals is used again.

The Lord Uses Suffering to Develop the Character of His People

Pain and suffering, though, are not always a result of poor choices made by us. Sometimes we suffer for no apparent reason. In fact, there are times when people do the right thing and then suffer for it.

One purpose pain and suffering can have in these cases is to be used by God to develop character in His people. Patience, endurance, and perseverance, for example, are qualities needed by the Lord's people, yet they do not come naturally. God's Word is filled with passages that teach His people to learn to wait on Him. Here are just some of the many examples:

Indeed, none who wait for you shall be put to shame; … (Psalm 25:3).

Lead me in your truth and teach me, for you are the God of my salvation; for you I wait all the day long (Psalm 25:5).

May integrity and uprightness preserve me, for I wait for you (Psalm 25:21).

Wait for the LORD; be strong, and let your heart take courage; wait for the LORD! (Psalm 27:14).

Be still before the LORD and wait patiently for him; … (Psalm 37:7).

For God alone my soul waits in silence; from him comes my salvation (Psalm 62:1).

O LORD, be gracious to us; we wait for you. Be our arm every morning, our salvation in the time of trouble (Isaiah 33:2).

Do not say, "I will repay evil"; wait for the LORD, and he will deliver you (Proverbs 20:22).

But as for me, I will look to the LORD; I will wait for the God of my salvation; my God will hear me (Micah 7:7).

We see that the common idea in these passages is that we should not run on ahead of the Lord and try to solve our problems our own way by our own devices. It is better to wait on the Lord and trust Him to be our help and our salvation in times of trouble. It takes patience to do this.

When our children were small, my wife and I would sometimes take them for a walk, and occasionally, they would run ahead of us. As we approached an intersection, we would have to remind them, "Stay behind us, let's cross together." It was a potentially dangerous situation, and they needed our help to handle it safely.

We, as God's children, constantly need His help and guidance to navigate the potentially dangerous events of life, but the problem is that we often lack the patience it takes to wait on Him.

God's Word teaches that suffering can have the effect of developing the patience within us that we need.

Count it all joy, my brothers, when you meet trials of various kinds, for you know that the testing of your faith produces steadfastness. And let steadfastness have its full effect, that you may be perfect and complete, lacking in nothing (James 1:2–4).

... we rejoice in our sufferings, knowing that suffering produces endurance, and endurance produces character, and character produces hope, and hope does not put us to shame, because God's love has been poured into our hearts through the Holy Spirit who has been given to us (Romans 5:3–5).

He wants us to experience a hope that does not disappoint or put us to shame. We see in the passage above that we walk in this kind of hope when we are properly relating to Him, when the Holy Spirit fills our hearts with His love, and when we have had our character developed through patiently enduring sufferings. When the Lord permits suffering to occur in our lives, it is not because He doesn't care, it is not because He is powerless; rather, it is because He loves us and wants to develop us into people who are of a proven character.

The Lord Uses Suffering to Test Our Faith

In his epistle, James states that God uses trials to test our faith.

Count it all joy, my brothers, when you meet trials of various kinds, for you know that the testing of your faith produces steadfastness. And let steadfastness have its full effect, that you may be perfect and complete, lacking in nothing (James 1:2–4).

Several years ago, my mother gave my wife various items of jewelry that she had acquired throughout her life. It was my wife's intention that we pass the jewelry on to our daughters so that these items would remain in the family as heirlooms. To divide the jewelry equally among all our daughters, we needed to know what each item was worth, and so we took them to a jeweler to have them appraised. If something is important to you, then you will probably want to know its true value.

How important to you is your faith in God? Is it worth having it appraised? If there is an area of your faith that needs development, would it not be best to have the Lord expose this and deal with it? The passage above says that He uses trials to do this. He does it so that we may be "perfect and complete, lacking in nothing."

The Lord is Pursuing the Maximum Harvest

One of the most famous forms of the lie of the ages is to raise the ancient question, "If God is good, just, and all powerful, then why does He allow some people to do very bad things to others?" In other words, "Why does He not intervene and bring judgment on the bad people right away, before they are allowed to cause additional harm?"

I believe that the Lord is never afraid of dealing with the questions that seem difficult to us. Jesus addressed this question with one of His parables that is recorded in Matthew, Chapter 13. It is the parable of the wheat and the weeds. Matthew records it this way:

> He put another parable before them, saying, "The kingdom of heaven may be compared to a man who sowed good seed in his field, but while his men were sleeping, his enemy came and sowed weeds among the wheat and went away. So when the plants came up and bore grain, then the weeds appeared also. And the servants of the master of the house came and said to him, 'Master, did you not sow good seed in your field? How then does it have weeds?' He said to them, 'An enemy has done this.' So the servants said to him, 'Then do you want us to go and gather them?' But he said, 'No, lest in gathering the weeds you root up the wheat along with them. Let both grow together until the harvest, and at harvest time I will tell the reapers, "Gather the weeds first and bind them in bundles to be burned, but gather the wheat into my barn"'" (Matthew 13:24–30).

There is debate, at times, concerning how to properly interpret some of the Lord's parables, but with this one there can be no doubt, because later in the chapter He gives the correct interpretation Himself. Here is what He says:

> He answered, "The one who sows the good seed is the Son of Man. The field is the world, and the good seed is the sons of the kingdom. The weeds are the sons of the evil one, and the enemy who sowed them is the devil. The harvest is the end of the age, and the reapers are angels. Just as the weeds are gathered and burned with fire, so will it be at the end of the age. The Son of Man will send his angels, and they will gather out of his kingdom all causes of sin and all law-breakers, and throw them into the fiery furnace. In that place there will be weeping and gnashing of teeth. Then the righteous will shine like the sun in the kingdom of their Father. He who has ears, let him hear" (Matthew 13:37–43).

Let us recap and draw some conclusions. The farmer represents the Lord; the wheat represents the Lord's people; the enemy represents the devil; and the weeds are the sons of the evil one. In other words, the weeds are the people who are under the influence of the devil. They are those who go around doing mean and wicked things to others. They are self-serving, driven by their own passions, and are disobedient to God. So why does God not just step into the scene and eliminate them right away? According to the parable, because if He did so, some of the wheat would be destroyed, as well.

How does that work? Why would some of the wheat be destroyed?

Look at it this way. Many people who are sons of the kingdom today were not always sons of the kingdom. There was a time when they were sons of the evil one, but they have since repented toward God and believed on the Lord Jesus Christ and called upon His name for salvation. Consider what Paul says to the Ephesians:

> Therefore remember that at one time you Gentiles in the flesh, called "the uncircumcision" by what is called the circumcision, which is made in the flesh by hands— remember that you were at that time separated from Christ, alienated from the commonwealth of Israel and strangers to the covenants of promise, having no hope and without God in the world. But now in Christ Jesus you who once were far off have been brought near by the blood of Christ (Ephesians 2:11–13).

And,

> for at one time you were darkness, but now you are light in the Lord … (Ephesians 5:8).

To this topic, Peter says the following:

> The Lord is not slow to fulfill his promise as some count slowness, but is patient toward you, not wishing that any should perish, but that all should reach repentance (2 Peter 3:9).

In other words, the Lord is patiently waiting before doing

perfect justice, so that more people will repent and turn to Him and experience His grace and forgiveness through faith in Jesus Christ, rather than experience His perfect justice.

Sometimes when people cry out for justice to be done to others, they do not understand the full extent of what this means. Are we, ourselves, ready to experience perfect justice? Or do we want justice for others, but grace and forgiveness for ourselves? It is easy to fall into such a trap.

Consider the plight of the early Jewish Christians suffering under the persecution that was led by Saul of Tarsus:

> … Saul was ravaging the church, and entering house after house, he dragged off men and women and committed them to prison (Acts 8:3).

And,

> But Saul, still breathing threats and murder against the disciples of the Lord, went to the high priest and asked him for letters to the synagogues at Damascus, so that if he found any belonging to the Way, men or women, he might bring them bound to Jerusalem (Acts 9:1–2).

Saul's persecution was harsh. He dragged both men and women off to prison and was even "breathing threats and murder" against any belonging to "the Way." What happened to the children of those families in which both the father and the mother were thrown into prison? No doubt, the people suffering under this persecution could have asked God, "Lord, why do you not stop this guy?" They could have been tempted to want justice to come and blast this Saul of Tarsus. But Jesus had a better way. He did stop Saul, but not with a blast of justice. It was a blast of grace.

If God would have blasted Saul right away with justice, how much wheat would have been lost in His kingdom? How many people heard the gospel through the preaching of the converted man who became Paul, the Apostle? How many churches were planted, and how many people have read the epistles he wrote, which now comprise almost half of the New Testament?

The Lord knows what He is doing. He is going for the maximum wheat harvest.

God Restores the Fortunes of His People

In this book we have been looking at the ways God uses suffering in the lives of His people. We have seen that sometimes we suffer because of foolish choices we have made, sometimes we suffer for no immediately apparent reason (at least, as far as we can see), but that God uses the suffering to refine us and to develop us into better people. We saw in earlier chapters that when Mary and Martha of Bethany called on the Lord for help, the Lord temporarily delayed in coming and led them deeper into pain and grief, so that they might experience a far richer blessing. Yet it would be a mistake to conclude that He always delays like this. The point to be made is not that the Lord always delays when we call for help, but that in those times when He does delay, He has a good reason.

The Bible teaches that God is a restorer of the fortunes of His people. While he does allow pain, suffering, and sometimes loss of treasure to occur, He invites His people to call upon Him in their trouble and promises to help them if they do.

> Oh, that salvation for Israel would come out of Zion! When God restores the fortunes of his people, let Jacob rejoice, let Israel be glad (Psalm 53:6).

> I will restore the fortunes of Judah and the fortunes of Israel, and rebuild them as they were at first (Jeremiah 33:7).

> Therefore thus says the Lord GOD: Now I will restore the fortunes of Jacob and have mercy on the whole house of Israel, and I will be jealous for my holy name (Ezekiel 39:25).

> "and call upon me in the day of trouble; I will deliver you, and you shall glorify me (Psalm 50:15).

The Lord is the restorer of the fortunes of His people. This statement has important implications. If God is the restorer of the fortunes of His people, then it means He, at times, will allow them to suffer loss of treasure. Some of the passages above are referring to restoring Judah after destruction and captivity were brought upon them by the Babylonian empire during the 7th and 6th centuries BC. God allowed the destruction and the captivity to occur, but then He restored their fortunes. We saw in the previous section about refinement the reason why He allowed the destruction and the captivity. It was a punishment for the sins of the people. Yet even though it was a punishment, He had benevolent intentions for the nation; He intended to purify them and to make them a nation that was eventually ready for the promised Messiah. He allowed the loss of treasure, but He did it with the view of making them a better people.

There are also times when the Lord allows the loss of treasure, not as a punishment, but simply to make His people more fruitful. Jesus taught about this on the night before His arrest, as He spoke preparing His disciples for what was coming.

> "I am the true vine, and my Father is the vinedresser. Every branch in me that does not bear fruit he takes away, and every branch that does bear fruit he prunes, that it may bear more fruit" (John 15:1–2).

Pruning involves the loss of something, and in the case of the vine, it is the loss of some of its branches. He removes them so that the remaining branches bear more fruit, so there is an overall net gain in the fruit produced. If He causes or allows His people to suffer loss, it is so He can later bring them to a greater blessing. Treasure may be lost. Yet He is a restorer of the fortunes of His people, and when the restoration occurs, it brings a greater blessing than the one that was originally lost.

God's Word teaches that He is our healer. It is characteristic of Him to provide help when people call upon Him for assistance. If God has allowed you to experience pain, grief, and loss, you can be sure that He will eventually provide healing and restoration; and frequently He will cause your last state to be better than the first. Sometimes this happens right away, but sometimes we must wait.

Sometimes we may have to wait until the new heavens and the new earth are established for the restoration to occur, but even if that is so, the restoration is certainly no less real. All who wait upon the Lord, trusting in Him, will not be disappointed.

While Jesus was physically present on earth doing ministry, it was characteristic of Him to help people who came to Him and asked for assistance. Whether it was the nobleman of John, Chapter 2; the paralytic of Matthew 8; a Roman centurion in Capernaum; Bartimaeus of Jericho; the woman with chronic bleeding; Jairus, the synagogue leader; or many others, they all received the help and healing they sought.

While He was in Capernaum, right after Jesus had just healed Peter's mother-in-law, Matthew writes:

> That evening they brought to him many who were oppressed by demons, and he cast out the spirits with a word and healed all who were sick. This was to fulfill what was spoken by the prophet Isaiah: "He took our illnesses and bore our diseases" (Matthew 8:16–17).

Peter, speaking of Jesus' ministry several years later, while preaching in the house of the Centurion named Cornelius, said of Him:

> … God anointed Jesus of Nazareth with the Holy Spirit and with power. He went about doing good and healing all who were oppressed by the devil, for God was with him. And we are witnesses of all that he did both in the country of the Jews and in Jerusalem … (Acts 10:38–39).

So, we see that it was characteristic of Jesus' ministry to heal and to help those who came to Him, appealing for assistance.

Chapter 10

God's Workmanship—Abraham

At this point, we will look through the Scriptures at some examples of the Lord working to develop His people. These are people of action-oriented faith, who stood for what was right and sought to honor the Lord, and yet things did not always go as they expected. Sometimes, circumstances developed that did not seem to make sense. This put their faith to the test. Yet I believe the Lord's intention for them all along was to develop them. Each one had faith and showed promise, but God's intention was to take them further in their walk of faith, and deeper into an intimate relationship with Himself.

Abraham had Faith in God

Abraham is one of the most often-used examples in all of Scripture of someone modeling a proper faith in God. He is mentioned by Moses, Isaiah, Nehemiah, Paul, the writer of Hebrews, and the Lord Jesus (just to name a few), as a friend of God and an example of faith. God called Abraham to leave his relatives and familiar surroundings to go to the land that He would show him (Genesis 12:1). Abraham obeyed. Hebrews, Chapter 11 says of him:

By faith Abraham obeyed when he was called to go out to a place that he was to receive as an inheritance. And he went out, not knowing where he was going. By faith he went to live in the land of promise, as in a foreign land, living in tents with Isaac and Jacob, heirs with him of the same promise. For he was looking forward to the city that has foundations, whose designer and builder is God (Hebrews 11:8–10).

It is difficult to leave your familiar surroundings, extended family, and friends, and go to a land where you do not know the language, customs, or people. Abraham did not even know for sure where he was going. He could not prepare ahead of time by asking others who may have been to this new place what the customs, language, and ways were like.

When my wife and I were first married, we served the first four and a half years of our married life together as missionaries in a country in South America. Even though we knew where we were going, and had both attended language school, it was difficult to make the transition. Crossing culture means relearning dozens of everyday subconscious habits that one takes for granted, but that no longer work in the new culture. It is hard work to adjust.

Abraham did not even have a permanent home in the new land. He lived in tents and moved about as a nomad. Yet he was willing to do this, because God had spoken to him and had given him a promise. It was an act of strong faith.

Even so, the Lord wanted to develop Abraham's faith further.

Earlier, I mentioned the parable of the vine and the vinedresser that Jesus told his disciples the night before His arrest.

I am the true vine, and my Father is the vinedresser. Every branch in me that does not bear fruit he takes away, and every branch that does bear fruit he prunes, that it may bear more fruit (John 15:1–2).

When the Lord's children bear good fruit, He will then work to develop them so that they might bear even more fruit. This was the case with Abraham.

The Lord Gave Abraham a Test

Abraham had already demonstrated faith by leaving his home and going to live as a foreigner in a different land, but God had in mind to develop his faith even further. So, we read in Genesis,

Chapter 22, the following:

> After these things God tested Abraham and said to him, "Abraham!" And he said, "Here I am." He said, "Take your son, your only son Isaac, whom you love, and go to the land of Moriah, and offer him there as a burnt offering on one of the mountains of which I shall tell you" (Genesis 22:1–2).

The command by God must have completely stunned Abraham. Isaac was his child of promise. This was his only son by his wife, Sarah. This was the child whom God had promised to give them before he was born, and through whom God would fulfill His other covenant promises. How could the Lord command this to happen and keep His word?

Abraham did not know how all of this would play out, but he knew what God had promised, and he knew what God had told him to do. He believed both God's promise and His command. So, he went.

Hebrews, Chapter 11, again gives us insight into what he was thinking:

> By faith Abraham, when he was tested, offered up Isaac, and he who had received the promises was in the act of offering up his only son, of whom it was said, "Through Isaac shall your offspring be named." He considered that God was able even to raise him from the dead, from which, figuratively speaking, he did receive him back (Hebrews 11:17–19).

Abraham had faith before he went to offer Isaac. We know this to be true. We know this because he went; he obeyed God. We know this because the writer of Hebrews tells us so. And we know this because of Abraham's own testimony as he approached Mount Moriah with Isaac.

> And Abraham took the wood of the burnt offering and laid it on Isaac his son. And he took in his hand the fire and the knife. So they went both of them together. And Isaac said to his father Abraham, "My father!" And he said, "Here I am, my son." He said, "Behold, the fire and the wood, but where

is the lamb for a burnt offering?" Abraham said, "God will provide for himself the lamb for a burnt offering, my son." So they went both of them together (Genesis 22:6–8).

Abraham's Faith Was Strengthened

Abraham's actions and his words indicate that he had a strong faith in God as he approached Mount Moriah with his son. The point I want to make is this: How much stronger was his faith and his trust in God when he returned from Mount Moriah, with his son alive, after having completely obeyed God? He went up the mount believing that he must obey God, that God would somehow provide the lamb, and that God would raise Isaac from the dead, if necessary, to keep His promise. He went through with it, believing God, and the Lord did not disappoint him.

> But the angel of the LORD called to him from heaven and said, "Abraham, Abraham!" And he said, "Here I am." He said, "Do not lay your hand on the boy or do anything to him, for now I know that you fear God, seeing you have not withheld your son, your only son, from me." And Abraham lifted up his eyes and looked, and behold, behind him was a ram, caught in a thicket by his horns. And Abraham went and took the ram and offered it up as a burnt offering instead of his son (Genesis 22:11–13).

After Abraham's obedient action, God said to him these words:

> ... "By Myself I have sworn, declares the LORD, because you have done this and have not withheld your son, your only son, I will surely bless you, and I will surely multiply your offspring as the stars of heaven and as the sand that is on the seashore. And your offspring shall possess the gate of his enemies, and in your offspring shall all the nations of the earth be blessed, because you have obeyed my voice (Genesis 22:16–18).

There are very few places in all of Scripture where God, Himself, takes an oath, and this is one of them. Abraham, indeed, received here a tremendous and weighty blessing, the full extent of which he may not have understood, but he knew that God had been faithful. He had trusted the Lord and was glad he did. I have to believe that when he walked down Mount Moriah, with the knowledge that he had fully obeyed the Lord, with a renewed promise from God, and with Isaac alive, that his faith in God was yet stronger.

James, speaking of Abraham and his offering of Isaac, states that Abraham's faith was made perfect through his obedient works. "You see that faith was working with his works, and as a result of the works, faith was perfected;" (James 2:22 NASB).

Though this incident was a very difficult and painful one for Abraham to walk through, God used it to develop his faith further. If Abraham had doubted God's good intentions, and chosen to believe the lie of the ages, instead of trusting the Lord, then he would not have been blessed in this way.

❧ Chapter 11 ❧

God's Workmanship—Job

Job has always been somewhat of a mysterious person to me. His book seems to stand by itself amid the other Old Testament books. Dr. Floyd Nolen Jones suggests the possibility that the book of Job is about the same man that is mentioned as Issachar's third son in Genesis 46:13, and therefore would have lived in the eighteenth century BC (Jones, p. 20). Several other commentators make no claim to know exactly who Job was, except to say that he was an actual historical man, rather than a symbolic fictional character, due to his being mentioned by Ezekiel and James (Andersen, p.78 and Easton, p. 391).

There are a few things we can conclude simply by reading the book of Job itself. For one thing, he had a large family. One wife is mentioned, as well as seven sons, three daughters, and many servants. We also know that he is described as having great wealth. Wealth in his time was not measured by money in the bank, but by possession of flocks, herds, and livestock. It was through these that one's provision and income-generation occurred. Job possessed 7,000 sheep, 3,000 camels, 500 yoke of oxen, and 500 female donkeys. He is described as the greatest man of all the people of the east (Job 1:3).

Having a blessed family and great material wealth did not lead Job to forget God. He continually prayed for and offered sacrifices for his family. God, Himself described Job as a "blameless and upright man, who fears God and turns away from evil" (Job 1:8). Because of this statement, we know that Job managed the affairs of his life well. This would include his dealings in business, family matters, and with neighbors. He had to have been honest, thorough, and to have treated people right for God to make this declaration. He also must have been a good husband and father, striking a healthy balance between work and family devotion. Reading through Chapter 1, we notice that his children enjoyed hosting meals for one another. They apparently enjoyed a warm fellowship with each other. Among wealthy families it is not uncommon to find bitter rivalries, competition, or jealousy, but these attitudes did not seem to be present among Job's family.

God Permitted Job to Be Tested

Everything was going quite well for Job, until one day there was a discussion about him in the spiritual realm.

> Now there was a day when the sons of God came to present themselves before the LORD, and Satan also came among them. The LORD said to Satan, "From where do you come?" Satan answered the LORD and said, "From roaming about on the earth and walking around on it." The LORD said to Satan, "Have you considered My servant Job? For there is no one like him on the earth, a blameless and upright man, fearing God and turning away from evil." Then Satan answered the LORD, "Does Job fear God for nothing? Have You not made a fence around him and his house and all that he has, on every side? You have blessed the work of his hands, and his possessions have increased in the land. But reach out with Your hand now and touch all that he has; he will certainly curse You to Your face." Then the LORD said to Satan, "Behold, all that he has is in your power, only do not reach out and put your hand on him." So Satan departed from the presence of the LORD (Job 1:6–12 NASB).

Satan, in this conversation, could not find anything about Job's conduct that would give him cause to accuse him, so he accused Job's motives. So, the Lord decided to allow a test to demonstrate that even Job's motives were upright. Satan was allowed to strip Job of his flocks, herds, and possessions, and to take the lives of his children, but was not allowed to touch Job himself.

One thing to note here is that God did not take any direct action against Job, but removed some of the hedge of protection, and this allowed Satan to attack. Satan, however, is not all powerful and could do no more than what the Lord permitted. Yet, the Lord did permit him to attack, and, as we shall see, had His own purpose for doing so.

After all this occurred, Job maintained his faith in God.

> Then Job arose and tore his robe and shaved his head and fell on the ground and worshiped. And he said, "Naked I came from my mother's womb, and naked shall I return. The LORD gave, and the LORD has taken away; blessed be the name of the LORD."
> In all this Job did not sin or charge God with wrong (Job 1:20-22).

It is necessary to pause here for a few minutes and think about what has just been described. Job's conduct was upright, so Satan accused his inner motives. God allowed him to be tested, and he passed the test with flying colors. After losing all his wealth, all his sons, and all his daughters, he grieved, tore his robe, fell, and worshiped the Lord! He stated that he knew God gave him everything, and he attributed God with removing everything, and yet he did not charge God with wrongdoing; but rather, worshiped Him.

Satan must have been very frustrated with the outcome of Job's test. The Lord, however, was pleased. The next time Satan came around to talk about Job, God repeated His previous statement that Job was a "blameless and upright man, who fears God and turns away from evil." But then this time, He added, "He still holds fast his integrity, although you incited me against him to destroy him without reason" (Job 2:3).

Satan again could not find fault with Job's conduct, and so again accused his motives, but this time in a different way (because Job's response to the suffering had blown away his last accusation). This time, he accused Job of being selfish. If he personally suffers in the flesh, then he will curse God to His face, or so the accusation goes.

Then Satan answered the LORD and said, "Skin for skin! All that a man has he will give for his life. But stretch out your hand and touch his bone and his flesh, and he will curse you to your face." And the LORD said to Satan, "Behold, he is in your hand; only spare his life" (Job 2:4–6).

Satan then struck Job with horrible sores all over his body from head to toe (Job 2:7).

This next point is a big one. Up to this point God had been pleased with Job's conduct, so Satan accused his motives, then God allowed Job to be tested, and Job responded extremely well to the test. Next, Satan accused his motives in a new way, and God then permitted him to be tested yet again. Even though the Lord was quite pleased with Job up to this point, His response (at least in part) to Job's doing well through the first test, was to give him another test. This is a point we must not miss. I believe that God clearly loved Job. He had Job's best interests at heart. Even so, once Job endured well through the first trial, he was given yet another one.

If we experience something that is difficult, something that causes weighty pain and grief, and come through it by faith in God, it does not follow that we will never experience any more trouble.

As we shall see shortly, God was working to take his servant, Job, a man who served Him well, and make him into yet a better man. He intended to take this good relationship that He had with this man and make it still better. It is similar to the method He used with Mary and Martha of Bethany. His intention was to bring Job into a process through which His name would be glorified, His relationship with Job brought to a new level, and the accusations of Satan destroyed and silenced for good.

Though Job's conduct and motives proved to be acceptable in the Lord's sight, he did have a problem that God was working to remove through these events. It comes out, in the conversations that follow, that Job had developed a measure of over-confidence in his past conduct.

Job Responded to His Friends with Questions for God

Some friends of Job learned all that had happened to him, gathered, and came to visit and comfort him (Job 2:11). At first, they simply tore their robes, wept, and sat with Job for seven days and nights. This was a good start. It is always better to have a few friends around when going through a difficult time.

When the seven days passed, Job made a statement in which he expressed great grief and cursed the day he was born (Job, Chapter 3). His friends were not able to endure such a statement without responding, and so, a lengthy dialogue ensued. The friends could not believe that anything bad could happen to someone unless that person had committed terrible sins, and so even though they did not know exactly what Job had done wrong, they brought accusations against him anyway.

Some of their accusations follow:

"Remember: who that was innocent ever perished?
    Or where were the upright cut off?
As I have seen, those who plow iniquity
    and sow trouble reap the same" (Job 4:7–8).

"Does God pervert justice?
    Or does the Almighty pervert the right?
If your children have sinned against him, he has delivered
    them into the hand of their transgression" (Job 8:3–4).

"… Know then that God exacts of you less than your guilt deserves" (Job 11:6).

"Behold, God puts no trust in his holy ones,
    and the heavens are not pure in his sight;
how much less one who is abominable and corrupt,
    a man who drinks injustice like water!" (Job 15:15–16).

"Indeed, the light of the wicked is put out,
    and the flame of his fire does not shine" (Job 18:5).

"For he has crushed and abandoned the poor;
    he has seized a house that he did not build.
Because he knew no contentment in his belly,
    he will not let anything in which he delights escape him.
There was nothing left after he had eaten;
    therefore his prosperity will not endure" (Job 20:19–21).

Keep in mind that God had said that Job was upright, blameless, a man who feared God and turned away from evil. Even Satan could only accuse his motives. Yet these friends of Job had him supposedly sowing iniquity, drinking injustice like water, crushing and oppressing the poor, and even claimed that his children had died because they had sinned, too.

Job responded by maintaining his innocence. As he responded, there were some things that he knew for sure. He knew that he had not committed these offenses of which he had been accused by his acquaintances.

"Teach me, and I will be silent; make me understand how I
    have gone astray" (Job 6:24).

"I am a laughingstock to my friends;
    I, who called to God and he answered me,
    a just and blameless man, am a laughingstock."
                        (Job 12:4)

Yes, there were a few things that Job knew as he considered his plight, but there were also some things that he did not know. He did not know why he was suffering. He knew nothing of the conversation between God and Satan in the spiritual realm; he did not know of Satan's accusations or why God had permitted all these things to happen to him.

So, he said things like these:

"I will say to God, Do not condemn me;
    let me know why you contend against me.
Does it seem good to you to oppress,
    to despise the work of your hands

and favor the designs of the wicked?
Have you eyes of flesh?
   Do you see as man sees?
Are your days as the days of man,
   or your years as a man's years,
that you seek out my iniquity
   and search for my sin,
although you know that I am not guilty,
   and there is none to deliver out of your hand?"
(Job 10:2–7)

God Had Some Questions for Job

After the dialogue between Job and his acquaintances, the Lord appeared to Job during a storm and spoke to him. God's response to Job tells us that He saw that Job needed to be reminded that he did not know as much as he might have thought he did.

"Who is this that darkens counsel by words without
   knowledge?
Dress for action like a man;
   I will question you, and you make it known to me.
Where were you when I laid the foundation of the earth?
   Tell me, if you have understanding.
Who determined its measurements—surely you know!
   Or who stretched the line upon it?
On what were its bases sunk,
   or who laid its cornerstone,
when the morning stars sang together
   and all the sons of God shouted for joy?"
(Job 38:2–7)

The Lord's line of questioning reveals that He saw that Job had trusted too much in what he thought he knew, and that he did not know as much as he had supposed. God goes on to describe many aspects of nature and the creation's design, and to ask Job what he knew about them. The conclusion is obvious. Job had neither the power nor the knowledge to be in any position to evaluate God's performance in dealing with His creation.

God also addresses the issue of righteousness, saying, "Will you even put me in the wrong? Will you condemn me that you may be in the right?" (Job 40:8). Job did not possess the authority or the righteousness to judge God, but God does possess both the authority and the righteousness to judge him.

Job's response is appropriate:

Then Job answered the LORD and said:
   "Behold, I am of small account; what shall I answer you?
     I lay my hand on my mouth.
   I have spoken once, and I will not answer;
     twice, but I will proceed no further" (Job 40:3–5).

And,

Then Job answered the LORD and said:

   "I know that you can do all things,
     and that no purpose of yours can be thwarted.
   'Who is this that hides counsel without knowledge?'
   Therefore I have uttered what I did not understand,
     things too wonderful for me, which I did not know.
   'Hear, and I will speak;
     I will question you, and you make it known to me.'
   I had heard of you by the hearing of the ear,
     but now my eye sees you;
   therefore I despise myself,
     and repent in dust and ashes" (Job 42:1–6).

Even though Job had questioned what God was doing, Satan's accusations about him proved to be false. When God appeared to him, Job did not curse Him to His face. Rather, he humbled himself before his Maker. Throughout his trials, Job maintained a foundational faith in God, even though he did not understand why he was going through such trouble.

   "Though he slay me, I will hope in him; yet I will argue my
     ways to his face (Job 13:15).

   "For I know that my Redeemer lives,

and at the last he will stand upon the earth.
  And after my skin has been thus destroyed,
    yet in my flesh I shall see God,
  whom I shall see for myself,
    and my eyes shall behold, and not another.
    My heart faints within me!" (Job 19:25–27).

God Restored Job's Fortunes

As we have seen in earlier chapters, when the Lord brings his people through trials and affliction, he will eventually restore their fortunes. This was Job's experience when he had humbled himself before God.

> And the LORD restored the fortunes of Job, when he had prayed for his friends. And the LORD gave Job twice as much as he had before. Then came to him all his brothers and sisters and all who had known him before, and ate bread with him in his house. And they showed him sympathy and comforted him for all the evil that the LORD had brought upon him. And each of them gave him a piece of money and a ring of gold.

> And the LORD blessed the latter days of Job more than his beginning. And he had 14,000 sheep, 6,000 camels, 1,000 yoke of oxen, and 1,000 female donkeys. He had also seven sons and three daughters (Job 42:10–13).

God took a basically good man and made him better. He took a man who had been richly blessed and positioned him to be blessed even more. He took a man that He could call blameless, and brought that man through a series of events, painful though they be, that were used to develop that man into a man with still greater character. Through these trials Job became humbler and more aware of God's infinitely superior knowledge, power, and righteousness. Job became a man with a deeper faith; and therefore, a far richer fellowship with his God.

The book of Job does not record that God ever told Job, at least in this life, why the suffering had happened. Yet we, the readers of his book, know that God used these events to develop Job, to silence the accusations of Satan, and to glorify His name. Job simply had to trust that the Lord knew things that he did not, and that He had his best interests at heart.

Chapter 12

God's Workmanship—Joseph

So far, we have seen in the cases of Abraham and Job that God used pain and grief to further develop their faith and character, and to take their relationships to a higher level. Next, we will look at the Lord's dealings with Joseph. In Joseph's case, the Lord not only works to develop him, but an additional dynamic is brought into play, as well. To see what that dynamic is, we must first review the events that led up to it.

Genesis devotes fourteen chapters to the events in Joseph's life, so the best I can do here is summarize. While Joseph's birth is recorded in Genesis, Chapter 30, the narrative of his life begins in Chapter 37 and continues to the end of Genesis, through Chapter 50.

Joseph's Story

To understand the dynamics at work in Joseph's life, one must first understand a few things about his family. Joseph's father is Jacob, and Jacob was a man who had four wives. Though this is true, it appears as though it was not Jacob's original intention to have more than one wife.

Jacob loved Rachel, the daughter of his uncle, Laban. So, he asked Laban to give him Rachel as a wife.

Jacob loved Rachel. And he said, "I will serve you seven years for your younger daughter Rachel. Laban said, "It is better that I give her to you than that I should give her to any other man; stay with me." So Jacob served seven years for Rachel, and they seemed to him but a few days because of the love he had for her (Genesis 29:18–20).

Jacob's love was for Rachel, and the woman he wanted to have as his wife was Rachel. Laban, nevertheless, tricked him and gave him his older daughter, Leah, instead, and then said that Jacob had to serve him another seven years if he wanted to marry Rachel, as well. Laban gave each daughter a female servant when the daughters were given in marriage to Jacob.

Jacob now had a family consisting of two wives, and each wife had a female servant. Jacob originally only wanted to marry Rachel, and the Scripture states plainly that he loved her more than her sister, Leah (Genesis 29:30).

When the Lord saw that Jacob loved Rachel, but that Leah was unloved, He caused Leah to begin to conceive and to have sons (Genesis 29:31). Leah, therefore, gave birth to Reuben, Simeon, Levi, and Judah, the first four sons of Jacob. Rachel then became envious of her sister because Leah was having children and she was not.

> ... She said to Jacob, "Give me children, or I shall die!" Jacob's anger was kindled against Rachel, and he said, "Am I in the place of God, who has withheld from you the fruit of the womb?" (Genesis 30:1–2).

Rachel then decided to give Bilhah, her servant, to Jacob as an additional wife, with the idea that she would have children through her. Jacob agreed to this and Bilhah had two sons, Dan and Naphtali.

With the competition apparently being quite fierce between the two sisters, Leah began to worry because she had stopped having children. Leah imitated the strategy of Rachel, and gave her servant, Zilpah, to Jacob as a wife. Zilpah then gave birth to Gad and Asher. Next, Leah had two more sons of her own, Issachar and Zebulun, plus a daughter, whom she named Dinah.

At this point in the narrative, Jacob had six sons and a daughter by Leah; two sons by Bilhah; two sons by Zilpah; but no children with Rachel, the woman he originally wanted to marry.

Then the Scripture says that the Lord remembered Rachel.

> Then God remembered Rachel, and God listened to her and opened her womb. She conceived and bore a son and said, "God has taken away my reproach." And she called his name Joseph, saying, "May the LORD add to me another son!" (Genesis 30:22–24).

Rachel finally had a son; he was named Joseph. Joseph was born into a situation in which his mother was loved more than the other wives, and there was intense competition between the women in the family. This competition would naturally filter down to the children and form a dynamic that was ripe for trouble. To make matters even worse, Jacob (renamed Israel by God) loved Joseph more than the other children.

> Now Israel loved Joseph more than any other of his sons, because he was the son of his old age. And he made him a robe of many colors. But when his brothers saw that their father loved him more than all his brothers, they hated him and could not speak peacefully to him (Genesis 37:3–4).

It is obvious from their reaction that his brothers knew that the special robe meant that Joseph was a favored child. They could not even speak peacefully to him.

One additional factor that played into the troubled relationship between Joseph and his brothers was that, after tending flocks in the field with the sons of Bilhah and Zilpah, he brought a bad report of them to his father. It is a very natural reaction (though not a very godly one) to despise someone who does their job well, and who then reports you to your authority when you do not.

The situation had already developed into something quite volatile, when a new dynamic came into play that was like touching a match to a powder keg. Joseph began to have dreams. The dreams were of a nature that showed Joseph was to reign over the others. Joseph was not shy about sharing these dreams with his brothers.

> Now Joseph had a dream, and when he told it to his brothers they hated him even more. He said to them, "Hear this dream

that I have dreamed: Behold, we were binding sheaves in the field, and behold, my sheaf arose and stood upright. And behold, your sheaves gathered around it and bowed down to my sheaf. His brothers said to him, "Are you indeed to reign over us? Or are you indeed to rule over us?" So they hated him even more for his dreams and for his words (Genesis 37:5–8).

Twice this passage states that they hated him even more because he told them this dream. One question that may come to mind is, *Why even tell them this dream, when the relationship is already pretty strained?* One possibility is that Joseph already knew that the dream was from God, and that he had a responsibility to share it. In any case, he *did* share it.

Later, he had another similar dream. This time, it involved his parents as well as his brothers, and again, he shared the dream with his family. Jacob's reaction was mixed.

… when he told it to his father and to his brothers, his father rebuked him and said to him, "What is this dream that you have dreamed? Shall I and your mother and your brothers indeed come to bow ourselves to the ground before you?"

And his brothers were jealous of him, but his father kept the saying in mind (Genesis 37:9–11).

Jacob rebuked Joseph, but the text says that he kept the saying in mind. As far as the brothers were concerned, however, this was the last straw. As Joseph came out to visit them in the fields, they began to plot rather unseemly methods for dealing with him.

They saw him from afar, and before he came near to them they conspired against him to kill him. They said to one another, "Here comes this dreamer. Come now, let us kill him and throw him into one of the pits. Then we will say that a fierce animal has devoured him, and we will see what will become of his dreams" (Genesis 37:18–20).

Some of the brothers were ready to kill Joseph, but Reuben was not willing to go along with the plan and suggested that they put him in one of the nearby pits in the wilderness, with the idea that he would come by later and get Joseph out (Genesis 37:22).

While Reuben was away, Judah came up with the idea to sell Joseph as a slave to a group of travelers who were passing by. The other brothers agreed, and Joseph was sold (Genesis 37:25–28).

Joseph was taken to Egypt and sold as a slave to a man named Potiphar, who was the Pharaoh's captain of the guard (Genesis 37:36). Even though Joseph was a slave at that point, God began to prosper all that he touched.

> The LORD was with Joseph, and he became a successful man, and he was in the house of his Egyptian master. His master saw that the LORD was with him and that the LORD caused all that he did to succeed in his hands. So Joseph found favor in his sight and attended him, and he made him overseer of his house and put him in charge of all that he had. From the time that he made him overseer in his house and over all that he had, the LORD blessed the Egyptian's house for Joseph's sake; the blessing of the LORD was on all that he had, in house and field. So he left all that he had in Joseph's charge, and because of him he had no concern about anything but the food he ate (Genesis 39:2–6).

At that point, though he was a slave, things seemed to be going fairly well for Joseph. He was a high-ranking servant and oversaw everything that Potiphar owned. Then things took another dark turn.

Potiphar's wife noticed that Joseph was quite handsome and began to make repeated sexual advances toward him. Joseph refused over and over again, and finally ran away from her, leaving her holding his garment. She invented a story, and falsely accused Joseph of attempting to sexually assault her (Genesis 39:7–18). As soon as Potiphar heard of it, he became furious and had Joseph thrown into the king's prison (Genesis 39:19–20).

Joseph's Response

By this time, Joseph had many factors tempting him to doubt that God had his best interests at heart. Few people have had more apparent reason to give in to the lie of the ages than Joseph did at this point in his life. He did not ask to be born into a family that was already filled with competition and strife; he did not ask to be his father's favorite child; he did not ask to be given the prophetic dreams; he did not ask to be sold as a slave; and he certainly did not deserve to be falsely accused and thrown into the king's prison. By now he could be asking, "God, what are You doing to me?!" It is quite likely that tempting spirits were whispering into his ear, "If God is so great and is *for* you, then why are you here? Why have all these things happened to you?"

Joseph, though, did not give in to this temptation any more than he gave in to the temptations presented by Potiphar's wife. Rather, he continued to serve God while in prison.

> But the LORD was with Joseph and showed him steadfast love and gave him favor in the sight of the keeper of the prison. And the keeper of the prison put Joseph in charge of all the prisoners who were in the prison. Whatever was done there, he was the one who did it. The keeper of the prison paid no attention to anything that was in Joseph's charge, because the LORD was with him. And whatever he did, the LORD made it succeed (Genesis 39:21–23).

God knew that it was not fun to be sold into slavery, and He knew that it was not enjoyable to be falsely accused and thrown into the king's prison. Yet when these things happened to Joseph, it did not mean that God was not with him. Clearly, He was. He granted Joseph grace in the sight of his overseers wherever Joseph went and caused all that he did to prosper. Joseph may not have known why all these things were happening to him, but the Lord knew exactly what He was doing. He was working out His plan.

God's Plan

The remainder of the chapters in the book of Genesis go on to describe how God worked out His plan in the life of Joseph. Joseph interpreted the dreams of a couple of the fellow prisoners, and this ultimately led to his interpreting a dream for Pharaoh, the king of Egypt. Pharaoh then freed Joseph from prison and exalted him to the level of second in command in all of Egypt. The interpretation warned Pharaoh and all of Egypt of a coming famine so that they could prepare properly for it through the wisdom that God gave Joseph. When the famine hit, Joseph's family learned that there was food in Egypt, and so Jacob sent Joseph's brothers there to buy food. After first testing his brothers, Joseph eventually revealed himself to them, and they were all reconciled. Jacob learned of all this, and at Joseph's invitation, moved his entire family to Egypt.

In the beginning, it may have looked to Joseph as if all things were spinning out of control. He was hated by his brothers; he was sold as a slave; he was dragged to a strange land away from his family; he was falsely accused; and he was cast into prison. God, however, was not only using these unpleasant events to develop Joseph's own character and faith, but was working out a plan to save the lives of probably millions of people in Egypt, and Joseph's own family, as well. Through Joseph's suffering many lives were saved.

When Jacob died while living in Egypt, Joseph's brothers worried that maybe he had not really forgiven them and was only acting nice toward them for Jacob's sake. Joseph, after all, was second in command of all of Egypt. His word was law. He could have had his brothers punished or even executed at any time by just saying the word. So, they prepared a message for him.

> When Joseph's brothers saw that their father was dead, they said, "It may be that Joseph will hate us and pay us back for all the evil that we did to him." So they sent a message to Joseph, saying, "Your father gave this command before he died: 'Say to Joseph, "Please forgive the transgression of your brothers and their sin, because they did evil to you."' And now, please forgive the transgression of the servants of the God of your father" ... (Genesis 50:15–17).

Joseph's response showed that he had not believed the lie of the ages, and he was not bitter or unforgiving toward his brothers.

> … Joseph wept when they spoke to him (Genesis 50:17).

And,

> But Joseph said to them, "Do not fear, for am I in the place of God? As for you, you meant evil against me, but God meant it for good, to bring it about that many people should be kept alive, as they are today. So do not fear; I will provide for you and your little ones." Thus he comforted them and spoke kindly to them (Genesis 50:19–21).

Joseph was not bitter with God or with his brothers. He could see that God had a plan to work out all along. Yes, his brothers meant evil against him, and he recognized this to be true. However, he also recognized that he was not God, and that only God is in the proper position to judge and/or punish his brothers. As the events in the early days of Joseph's life were unfolding, God had intentions that neither he nor his brothers knew anything about, and these intentions were good. God had Joseph's best interests at heart all along.

Chapter 13

God's Workmanship—
Hezekiah

Next, we will look at Hezekiah, one of the kings of Judah. Hezekiah began to reign late in the eighth century B.C. (approximately 726 B.C., according to Dr. Jones' chronology—Jones, p. 167). To understand Hezekiah's situation, we first need to know some things about his upbringing.

Hezekiah grew up in a time when the children of Israel were divided into two kingdoms, the northern and the southern. A looming threat at that time was the growing power of the nation of Assyria.

Hezekiah's Father Did Not Serve God

Hezekiah's father was King Ahaz, who ruled Judah, the southern kingdom, from Jerusalem for sixteen years (2 Kings 16:2). Ahaz set a bad example for his son Hezekiah in several ways; he is described by the writer of 2 Kings as not doing what was right in the eyes of the Lord.

> ... And he did not do what was right in the eyes of the LORD his God, as his father David had done, but he walked in the way of the kings of Israel. He even burned his son as an offering, according to the despicable practices of the nations whom the LORD drove out before the people of Israel. And he sacrificed and made offerings on the high places and on the hills and under every green tree (2 Kings 16:2–4).

Ahaz disobeyed the Lord in his politics, as well. Isaiah, the prophet, had warned him against forming an alliance with the king of Assyria (Isaiah, Chapters 7 and 8), but according to Old Testament scholar Leon Wood, Ahaz was pro-Assyrian in his politics "from the beginning of his reign." (Wood, p. 355)

Detecting Ahaz's pro-Assyrian stance, the northern kingdom of Israel, led at the time by King Pekah, formed an alliance with the nation of Syria and together they came against Ahaz (2 Kings 16:5 and 2 Chronicles 28:5–8). Edom and the Philistines also attacked and caused trouble for Judah because of the errant leadership of King Ahaz (2 Chronicles 28:16–19).

Instead of looking to the Lord for help during the time of his trials, Ahaz turned to Assyria (2 Chronicles 28:16) and to false gods.

> In the time of his distress he became yet more faithless to the LORD—this same King Ahaz. For he sacrificed to the gods of Damascus that had defeated him and said, "Because the gods of the kings of Syria helped them, I will sacrifice to them that they may help me." But they were the ruin of him and of all Israel (2 Chronicles 28:22–23).

He not only turned to the false gods, but he also disrupted and opposed the proper worship of God.

> And Ahaz gathered together the vessels of the house of God and cut in pieces the vessels of the house of God, and he shut up the doors of the house of the LORD, and he made himself altars in every corner of Jerusalem. In every city of Judah he made high places to make offerings to other gods, provoking to anger the LORD, the God of his fathers (2 Chronicles 28:24–25).

This was the example of Hezekiah's father, King Ahaz.

Hezekiah's Zeal for the Lord

Hezekiah, however, was determined to not follow the poor example his father had given him. The description of his reign by the writer of 2 Kings is highly complimentary.

And he did what was right in the eyes of the LORD, according to all that David his father had done.

He trusted in the LORD, the God of Israel, so that there was none like him among all the kings of Judah after him, nor among those who were before him. For he held fast to the LORD. He did not depart from following him, but kept the commandments that the LORD commanded Moses (2 Kings 18:3 and 5–6).

In regard to this description of Hezekiah's reign, Leon Wood writes,

Hezekiah was one of Judah's finest kings in the sight of God. He is given the high accolade of having acted as David his father, and also of being the peer of all Judah's kings in trusting God (2 Kings 18:5). After the deliberate idolatry of Ahaz, drastic reform was necessary, and Hezekiah effected it (Wood, p. 357).

Once his reign began, Hezekiah wasted no time in restoring proper worship of the living God. In the first month of the first year of his reign, he opened the doors of the temple of God, and repaired them (2 Chronicles 29:3). He immediately ordered the temple to be cleansed of the filth that his father had brought into it, and as soon as that work was completed (in about two weeks), he began restoring proper worship (2 Chronicles 29:4–17).

Here is a list of actions he took to honor God:

- He repaired the temple doors (2 Chronicles 29:3).

- He had the temple cleaned out right away (2 Chronicles 29:3–19).

- He restored proper worship, involving the sons of Heman, Asaph, and of the Kohathites. To these he gave the job of cleansing the temple (2 Chronicles 29:12–19, 25).

- He restored proper sacrifices in the temple as soon as it was cleansed (2 Chronicles 29:20–36).

- He organized and celebrated a great Passover feast inviting all Israel, including the tribes from the northern kingdom (2 Chronicles 30:1-27).

- He broke down the idols throughout Judah, Benjamin, Ephraim, and Manasseh, until he destroyed them all (2 Chronicles 31:1).

- He organized the priests (2 Chronicles 31:2).

- He provided sacrifices from his own possessions (2 Chronicles 31:3).

- Restored proper tithing of the people to supply for the priests and the Levites (2 Chronicles 31:4–10).

Regarding the Passover feast that Hezekiah set up, this event took an enormous amount of effort and planning. All of Israel was invited, even the tribes of the northern kingdom. Some of the people of the northern kingdom scoffed at Hezekiah's couriers and mocked them; nevertheless, they faithfully carried out their mission (2 Chronicles 30:10). Yet there were those who "humbled themselves and came to Jerusalem" for the celebration (2 Chronicles 30:11). The result was phenomenal.

> So there was great joy in Jerusalem, for since the time of Solomon the son of David king of Israel there had been nothing like this in Jerusalem. Then the priests and the Levites arose and blessed the people, and their voice was heard, and their prayer came to his holy habitation in heaven (2 Chronicles 30:26–27).

Despite being raised by a father who was determined to ignore and offend the living God, Hezekiah was fully devoted to actively honoring God. Here is an inspired summary of Hezekiah's reforms:

> Thus Hezekiah did throughout all Judah, and he did what was good and right and faithful before the LORD his God. And every work that he undertook in the service of the house of God and in accordance with the law and the commandments, seeking his God, he did with all his heart, and prospered (2 Chronicles 31:20–21).

Troubling Times

After this level of demonstrated devotion to the Lord, one might think that God would bless and prosper Hezekiah's reign continually. And for the most part, He did. Not long, however, after these reforms were instituted, the Assyrians came and began to attack the fortified cities of Judah. Samaria, the seat of the northern kingdom of Israel, fell to the Assyrians while Hezekiah was reigning in Jerusalem (2 Kings 18:10), and they began to move on the fortified cities of Hezekiah's territory only a few years later (2 Kings 18:13). Many people, if found in Hezekiah's situation, would think to themselves, *What is this? After all the effort I have put into restoring the worship and the honor of the Lord, He allows these Assyrians to march into our land and take our fortified cities? Why?*

Even the writer of 2 Chronicles seems to anticipate the question. He writes,

After these things and these acts of faithfulness, Sennacherib king of Assyria came and invaded Judah and encamped against the fortified cities, thinking to win them for himself (2 Chronicles 32:1).

It could seem to some as though God responded to Hezekiah's good efforts by sending him trouble. The lie of the ages would say to Hezekiah, "See, your God does not really care about you! You instituted all these reforms, and look, the Assyrians are coming and attacking your land anyway."

Hezekiah's Response

When considering Hezekiah's overall response, he did not succumb to the temptation to believe the lie of the ages. He did all that he humanly could to resist the Assyrians, but he also prayed to his God for help and deliverance. Most of his actions demonstrate that he had a deep faith in God.

His initial response, however, was probably not his best. He sent a message to the king of Assyria apologizing for his previous resistance and began to pay tribute. He even stripped gold from the temple doors to pay what Sennacherib, the king of Assyria, required (2 Kings 18:14–16). I personally believe that this was a mistake. God did not need for him to strip gold from the doors of the temple for Him to deliver Jerusalem from the hand of Sennacherib. In any case, it did not work for very long. 2 Kings 18:17 records that Sennacherib sent his army commanders to Jerusalem to demand Jerusalem's unconditional surrender.

The paying of the tribute was not, however, Hezekiah's only response. When Hezekiah saw that the Assyrians were moving into Judah to take her fortified cities, he took several defensive measures. 2 Chronicles, Chapter 32, verses 2–8 describe these actions:

- He met with his officials and together they planned their response.

- He stopped up the wells, springs, and brooks outside of Jerusalem so that the invading armies could not use them for fresh water supplies.

- He built stronger walls around Jerusalem and raised up towers along them to increase the defensive position of his city.

- He made weapons and shields "in abundance" for the people of Jerusalem to use.

- He placed combat commanders over the people.

- He gathered them together and spoke to encourage them for what they were about to face.

"Be strong and courageous. Do not be afraid or dismayed before the king of Assyria and all the horde that is with him, for there are more with us than with him. With him is an arm of flesh, but with us is the LORD our God, to help us and to fight our battles." And the people took confidence from the words of Hezekiah king of Judah (2 Chronicles 32:7–8).

So instead of believing the lie of the ages, and throwing his hands up in defeat, Hezekiah acted, and encouraged his people. He did what he humanly could do for his defense. Yet, as we shall see, that is not all he did. He also prayed to the living God.

I have known of people who, when facing a problem, believe that they should respond by praying to God (which is good, prayer to God is a demonstration of faith and trust in Him), but then they do not take any action to help themselves through the situation. They have the idea that they will ask God for help, and then for their part they will sit and do nothing; because, in their mind, to try to help themselves is somehow viewed as lacking faith in what God will do. Hezekiah did not take this stance. When he saw the threat against his people, he prayed fervently, but he also did what was in his power to do as king to defend his people and meet the threat. He trusted in God, prayed to God, and acted in faith.

Jesus, when teaching His followers to pray, said these words:

"Ask, and it will be given to you; seek, and you will find; knock, and it will be opened to you. For everyone who asks receives, and the one who seeks finds, and to the one who knocks it will be opened" (Matthew 7:7-8).

The pattern presented by the Lord is to trust God enough to ask in prayer for what you need, and then to trust God enough to act on what you have prayed. This is what Hezekiah did. He trusted God enough to pray for help, he took such action as he could to meet the threat, and he trusted God to do what he could not do himself.

Sennacherib's Boast

The book of Proverbs warns of the dangers of pride:

When pride comes, then comes disgrace, but with the humble is wisdom (Proverbs 11:2).

And,

Pride goes before destruction, and a haughty spirit before a fall (Proverbs 16:18).

Sennacherib, however, was apparently not familiar with these words. He rolled into Judah intent on destroying it, and thinking that Jerusalem and her God were the same as all the cities and idols he had previously defeated. The message he sent to King Hezekiah and to the inhabitants of Jerusalem, demanding their unconditional surrender, reveals that he did not understand the nature of the real and living God whom Hezekiah served.

> Is Hezekiah not misleading you to give yourselves over to die by hunger and by thirst, saying, "The LORD our God will save us from the hand of the king of Assyria"? Is it not the same Hezekiah who removed His high places and His altars, and said to Judah and Jerusalem, "You shall worship before one altar, and on it you shall burn incense"? Do you not know what I and my fathers have done to all the peoples of the lands? Were the gods of the nations of those lands at all able to deliver their land from my hand? Who *was there* among all the gods of those nations which my fathers utterly destroyed who could deliver his people from my hand, that your God would be able to save you from my hand? Now then, do not let Hezekiah deceive you or mislead you like this, and do not believe him, for no god of any nation or kingdom was able to save his people from my hand or from the hand of my fathers. How much less will your God save you from my hand?" (2 Chronicles 32:11–15 NASB).

Sennacherib, here, made several important mistakes because he was not familiar with the nature of the living God of Israel. First, he assumed that when Hezekiah removed the idols from the "high places" that this was removing the legitimate places of worship of the God of Israel, and that this action had offended God. This was false. Sennacherib was obviously not familiar with the order of worship that God had established in the law of Moses, and therefore did not know what sort of worship pleased Him and what sort did not.

Secondly, he had become prideful and over-confident because of his previous success in battle. His trust was in his experience. We humans, all too often, tend to do this. We try something, and it seems to work, and so we try it again, and it seems to work again. After a while, trust can be falsely placed in our past accomplishments, and we can easily move forward with the same strategy, even though we are heading in a direction that the wisdom of God says not to take.

Finally, but not least, he grossly misunderstood what sort of God he was dealing with, and the power God was able to bring to bear on the situation. He was ignorant of the nature and the power of Hezekiah's God, and the results were devastating to him and to his army.

Hezekiah Prayed for Deliverance

The king of Assyria had marched on his land, threatened Jerusalem, and falsely accused Hezekiah of misleading and endangering the people. He tried to get the people to turn on Hezekiah as he attacked the city.

Hezekiah could have been angry with God; he could have believed the lie of the ages. He could have bitten his nails and cowered with fear. He could have just surrendered to the Assyrians, yet he did none of these things.

We already saw how he had taken such action as he humanly could take to prepare his city and his people for this moment. Then, when the message from Sennacherib came, he turned to God in intense prayer.

> Hezekiah prayed before the LORD and said, "LORD, God of Israel, enthroned *above* the cherubim, You are the God, You alone, of all the kingdoms of the earth. You have made heaven and earth. Incline Your ear, LORD, and hear; open Your eyes, LORD, and see; and listen to the words of Sennacherib, which he has sent to taunt the living God. It is true, LORD, the kings of Assyria have laid waste the nations and their lands, and have hurled their gods into the fire; for they were not gods but *only* the work of human hands, wood and stone. So they have destroyed them. But now, LORD our God, please, save us from his hand, so that all the kingdoms of the earth may know that You alone, LORD, are God" (2 Kings 19:15–19 NASB).

Hezekiah wanted to be saved from the Assyrians; he wanted the people of Jerusalem to be saved from the Assyrians; but he also wanted God to be glorified among the nations. He appealed for God to act so that, as he put it, *all the kingdoms of the earth may know that you, O Lord, are God alone.* Not only were their lives in danger, but, as Hezekiah saw it, God's reputation was at stake, because Sennacherib was boasting that no god, including the one real God, the God of Israel, could stop him. If Sennacherib were to succeed in destroying Jerusalem, it would look to the world as though the God whom Hezekiah served could not stop the Assyrians, especially after such a boast.

Hezekiah believed in his God. He wanted all the kingdoms to believe in his God, and he wanted Jerusalem to be saved. So, after doing all he humanly could do to strengthen his city, he appealed to the living God to act.

God did act. The first thing He did was send a message to Hezekiah, through the prophet Isaiah.

> "... Thus says the LORD, the God of Israel: Your prayer to me about Sennacherib king of Assyria I have heard."
> (2 Kings 19:20)

The Lord stated that Sennacherib's boasting against the God of Israel was not good (2 Kings 19:21–24), and that Sennacherib had failed to remember that God, Himself, had caused his military success until now, rather than his own strength or brilliance (2 Kings 19:25–26).

The Lord's message to Hezekiah and to Sennacherib was that Sennacherib would not succeed, and his boast would go completely and utterly refuted.

> Because you [Sennacherib] have raged against me and your complacency has come into my ears, I will put my hook in your nose and my bit in your mouth, and I will turn you back on the way by which you came (2 Kings 19:28).

Then the Lord took immediate action on this message which He had sent:

And that night the angel of the LORD went out and struck down 185,000 in the camp of the Assyrians. And when people arose early in the morning, behold, these were all dead bodies. Then Sennacherib king of Assyria departed and went home and lived at Nineveh (2 Kings 19:35–36).

Sennacherib's life had a sad ending. The Scriptures go on to relate that he returned to Nineveh with shame of face, and that his own sons assassinated him while he was worshiping in the temple of his god (2 Chronicles 32:21). Dr. Jones points out that, while the God of Israel was able to save Hezekiah from the onslaught of a massive army, Sennacherib's so-called god could not protect him even in the midst of its own temple (Jones, p. 169). His boasting against the real and living God had proved to be disastrous.

Hezekiah and Jerusalem, on the other hand, had been completely delivered from the life-threatening attack of a massive army. Rejecting the lies of the enemy and maintaining faith in the living God proved to be highly rewarding for both him and all the inhabitants of Jerusalem.

Hezekiah's Illness

The attack of the Assyrians was not the only life-threatening event that Hezekiah had to face. He also became very ill. 2 Kings, Chapter 20 says that he was even at the point of death. When Isaiah the prophet came to see him, instead of offering words of comfort, he stated plainly that God had revealed that Hezekiah was to die from the illness.

Until recently, I had always assumed that the illness came to Hezekiah after the threat from the Assyrians had passed, and that it was a subsequent event. After all, it is mentioned in the narratives of 2 Kings and 2 Chronicles after the writers completed their description of the Assyrian invasion. Yet when taking a little closer look at things, one can see that it was in the fourteenth year of Hezekiah's reign when the King of Assyria began to move against the fortified cities of Judah (2 Kings 18:13). Also, Isaiah said, after Hezekiah's prayer, that Hezekiah would live fifteen more years (2 Kings 20:6).

The biblical text mentions Hezekiah as reigning 29 years before he died (2 Kings 18:2 and 2 Chronicles 29:1), and so if one subtracts 15 from 29, that places the illness in the fourteenth year of Hezekiah's reign! This is, of course, the same year that Sennacherib began to move against the fortified cities of Judah. It appears, therefore, as though Hezekiah faced both life-threatening tests at the same time.

So, here is the King of Judah already dealing with the onslaught of the Assyrian invasion, and then he became ill as well.

What was a servant of God to do? Hezekiah responded to this threat in the same way that he responded to the Assyrian threat. He prayed to his God.

> Then Hezekiah turned his face to the wall and prayed to the LORD, saying, "Now, O LORD, please remember how I have walked before you in faithfulness and with a whole heart, and have done what is good in your sight." And Hezekiah wept bitterly (2 Kings 20:2–3).

Once again, the Lord responded to his prayer with action. Whereas God had originally told Isaiah to inform Hezekiah that he would die from this illness, He added fifteen more years to the king's life in response to this prayer. Here is what the Lord said,

> And before Isaiah had gone out of the middle court, the word of the LORD came to him: "Turn back, and say to Hezekiah the leader of my people, Thus says the LORD, the God of David your father: I have heard your prayer; I have seen your tears. Behold, I will heal you. On the third day you shall go up to the house of the LORD, and I will add fifteen years to your life. I will deliver you and this city out of the hand of the king of Assyria, and I will defend this city for my own sake and for my servant David's sake" (2 Kings 20:4-6).

Then the Lord confirmed His promise by miraculously causing the shadow on the steps of Ahaz to move backwards ten steps (2 Kings 20:9–11).

The Scripture states that Hezekiah had a problem with being

prideful (2 Chronicles 32:25–26), and so he certainly was not without his flaws of character. Nevertheless, when put to the test, he humbled himself and relied on God to see him through. Even though he had taken action to honor God and restore proper worship to the Kingdom of Judah, he was confronted with life-threatening trials; but rather than choose to believe the lie of the ages, he cried out in faith to his God, and the Lord heard his cry. Through these events, Hezekiah learned to lean on the strength of the Lord to get through his trials and glorified God in the process.

Chapter 14

God's Workmanship— Shadrach, Meshach, and Abednego

Even though the Lord had miraculously saved Jerusalem in the days of Hezekiah, it eventually came under the control of the Babylonian king a few generations later, because of the sin and the idolatry of the people (2 Kings 24:1–4). This began during the reign of Jehoiakim, King of Judah.

> In the third year of the reign of Jehoiakim king of Judah, Nebuchadnezzar king of Babylon came to Jerusalem and besieged it. And the Lord gave Jehoiakim king of Judah into his hand, with some of the vessels of the house of God. And he brought them to the land of Shinar, to the house of his god, and placed the vessels in the treasury of his god (Daniel 1:1–2).

Nebuchadnezzar not only carried away some of the vessels from the temple, but he took human prisoners as well, and carried them into the land of the Babylonians. He showed particular interest in the young people of royal family and of nobility, and placed them in a special training program so that they might be groomed to be attendants in his court (Daniel 1:3–5).

> Among these were Daniel, Hananiah, Mishael, and Azariah of the tribe of Judah. And the chief of the eunuchs gave them names: Daniel he called Belteshazzar, Hananiah he called Shadrach, Mishael he called Meshach, and Azariah he called Abednego (Daniel 1:6–7).

Shadrach, Meshach, and Abednego's story is found in the third chapter of the book of Daniel. After Nebuchadnezzar's recent military success, he apparently wanted to test the loyalty of his subjects. So, he set up an image of gold, gathered his various political officials to its dedication ceremony, and gave orders that whenever music was played they were to fall down and worship this image (Daniel 3:1–5).

Daniel does not seem to be present for this event. Possibly, his duties required him to be elsewhere at this time, but his three friends, Shadrach, Meshach, and Abednego were present, and they now had a problem. King Nebuchadnezzar had commanded everyone present to worship the image whenever the music was played, but the real and living God, the God of Israel had commanded His people not to bow down or worship any idols, images, or anything other than Himself (Exodus 20:1–5). Nebuchadnezzar had announced that anyone who refused to worship the golden image he had set up would be cast into a burning fiery furnace (Daniel 3:6).

Shadrach, Meshach, and Abednego had a choice to make. They could obey Nebuchadnezzar and bow down to worship the image, or they could obey God and refuse to do it. They could not do both.

Many people placed in a situation like this would find a reason to compromise. *How much could bowing down to an image just this one time really matter?* someone might think. *I don't really believe in that image; I'll just bow down this one time and avoid upsetting the king. After all, everyone else is doing it. They couldn't all be wrong, could they?*

Shadrach, Meshach, and Abednego did not think this way. They knew that God had clearly commanded one thing, and Nebuchadnezzar, king of Babylon, had clearly commanded the opposite thing, and that there was no way to obey them both. So, they chose to obey God, whatever the consequence might be. When the music was played, they did not bow down.

How they must have stood out as the music was played, and everyone bowed to the image except them. Imagine attending a worship service and the leader has everyone stand and join with him in prayer. All the people bow their heads and close their eyes.

Suppose the person leading in prayer continues for a while and your mind begins to wander. Suddenly, you realize that you have not been paying full attention; you look around, the prayer has ended, and everyone is seated except you. How embarrassing that would be! This is what it must have been like for Shadrach, Meshach, and Abednego, except they purposely choose to remain standing out of faithfulness to their God.

The stance they took did not go unnoticed.

Therefore at that time certain Chaldeans came forward and maliciously accused the Jews (Daniel 3:8).

"There are certain Jews whom you have appointed over the affairs of the province of Babylon: Shadrach, Meshach, and Abednego. These men, O king, pay no attention to you; they do not serve your gods or worship the golden image that you have set up" (Daniel 3:12).

King Nebuchadnezzar was furious. He immediately had these three men brought before him to investigate whether this accusation was true.

Nebuchadnezzar answered and said to them, "Is it true, O Shadrach, Meshach, and Abednego, that you do not serve my gods or worship the golden image that I have set up? Now if you are ready when you hear the sound of the horn, pipe, lyre, trigon, harp, bagpipe, and every kind of music, to fall down and worship the image that I have made, well and good. But if you do not worship, you shall immediately be cast into a burning fiery furnace. And who is the god who will deliver you out of my hands?" (Daniel 3:14–15).

Nebuchadnezzar obviously did not know the God of Israel. He thought that apart from the so-called gods that he served, there was no other god who was more powerful than he was himself. But he was about to find out the truth.

Just as Hezekiah did not want Sennacherib to succeed in conquering Jerusalem because it would bring dishonor to his God, so these three young Hebrews were willing to take any risk in order to ensure that their God was properly honored. The answer they gave to King Nebuchadnezzar remains classic.

> Shadrach, Meshach, and Abednego answered and said to the king, "O Nebuchadnezzar, we have no need to answer you in this matter. If this be so, our God whom we serve is able to deliver us from the burning fiery furnace, and he will deliver us out of your hand, O king. But if not, be it known to you, O king, that we will not serve your gods or worship the golden image that you have set up" (Daniel 3:16–18).

Let us take a minute just now to think about what these three fellows did here. At this point in history, Nebuchadnezzar was probably the most powerful king on the planet Earth. Daniel, when speaking to Belshazzar, a descendant of Nebuchadnezzar who became king after his days, said the following concerning Nebuchadnezzar and his power.

> O king, the Most High God gave Nebuchadnezzar your father kingship and greatness and glory and majesty. And because of the greatness that he gave him, all peoples, nations, and languages trembled and feared before him. Whom he would, he killed, and whom he would, he kept alive; whom he would, he raised up, and whom he would, he humbled (Daniel 5:18–19).

Such was the power and authority of Nebuchadnezzar. Shadrach, Meshach, and Abednego were aware of this and of whom it was that they were answering, but they did not waver in their faithfulness to the living God.

There is tremendous faith in God demonstrated in their answer. First, they affirmed that God was more powerful than Nebuchadnezzar and his false gods, being fully able to deliver them from his hand. Secondly, they confessed that they believed He would do it; they believed that God would take action to deliver them from King Nebuchadnezzar. Thirdly, they faithfully stated that even if God for some reason chose not to deliver them, they were still not going to worship the image or serve Nebuchadnezzar's gods. They would remain faithful to Him anyway. As far as believing in the God of Israel was concerned, they were all in. Whatever the consequences were going to be, they would not change their minds.

One could imagine that God would be very pleased with this answer. So much so, that He would immediately send his angels to their rescue and deliver Shadrach, Meshach, and Abednego from being cast into the fiery furnace. But that is not what He did. Despite their faithful answer, they were cast into the furnace.

Nebuchadnezzar became so angry with these three young men that he ordered the furnace to be heated seven times more than normal (Daniel 3:19).

> And he ordered some of the mighty men of his army to bind Shadrach, Meshach, and Abednego, and to cast them into the burning fiery furnace. Then these men were bound in their cloaks, their tunics, their hats, and their other garments, and they were thrown into the burning fiery furnace. Because the king's order was urgent and the furnace overheated, the flame of the fire killed those men who took up Shadrach, Meshach, and Abednego. And these three men, Shadrach, Meshach, and Abednego, fell bound into the burning fiery furnace (Daniel 3:20–23).

Sometimes we might be tempted to think, "If I serve God faithfully, and do what is right, then He will keep me from having to face trouble." Yet, these three men did serve God faithfully, and they gave the king the answer that they should have given, but they were still cast into the furnace.

Did God abandon them? Certainly not! Their story is not over yet.

Nebuchadnezzar quickly became astonished as he witnessed what took place next. They had cast three men bound into the furnace. The fire was so hot that it killed the soldiers who had thrown them in, but afterward he did not see three charred and burnt bodies in the furnace. Instead, he saw four men in the furnace; they were not bound, they were unharmed, and they were walking about. Nebuchadnezzar said that the appearance of the fourth was "like a son of the gods" (Daniel 3:24–25). People have differing opinions about the identity of the fourth person. Some say that it was an angel, and some say that it was the preincarnate Son of God. Whoever it was, God did not leave his faithful men unaccompanied in their difficult trial. Help was given to walk them through their fiery ordeal.

Nebuchadnezzar quickly ordered them out of the furnace.

"… Shadrach, Meshach, and Abednego, servants of the Most High God, come out, and come here!" Then Shadrach, Meshach, and Abednego came out from the fire. And the satraps, the prefects, the governors, and the king's counselors gathered together and saw that the fire had not had any power over the bodies of those men. The hair of their heads was not singed, their cloaks were not harmed, and no smell of fire had come upon them (Daniel 3:26–27).

These three young Hebrews had been miraculously rescued by God, though He had delayed a bit in doing so. This situation is like the one we discussed in earlier chapters when Jesus waited before coming to help Lazarus, His friend. The delay was not due to indifference or lack of power on God's part. He delayed so that He could do more, not less. If the Lord would have rescued these three before they were cast into the furnace, it would have been a good thing. But by waiting, allowing them to be cast in, and then bringing them through the furnace, it was a bigger thing, and brought more glory to the living God.

Before they were cast in the furnace, Nebuchadnezzar was very angry with Shadrach, Meshach, and Abednego. They were nothing more than furnace fuel to him. Afterward, he calls them "servants of the Most High God" (Daniel 3:26). Beforehand, the event was all about glorifying Nebuchadnezzar and his gods and bowing down to the image he had set up; afterward, Nebuchadnezzar glorified the real God and ordered everyone else to do so, as well!

Nebuchadnezzar answered and said, "Blessed be the God of Shadrach, Meshach, and Abednego, who has sent his angel and delivered his servants, who trusted in him, and set aside the king's command, and yielded up their bodies rather than serve and worship any god except their own God. Therefore I make a decree: Any people, nation, or language that speaks anything against the God of Shadrach, Meshach, and Abednego shall be torn limb from limb, and their houses laid in ruins, for there is no other god who is able to rescue in this way" (Daniel 3:28–29).

Whenever we go through trials that are used by God to glorify His name, it benefits us and the people around us. The nature of our God is not selfish. Shadrach, Meshach, and Abednego were promoted in the province of Babylon (Daniel 3:30); grew in their closeness to God through this event; were used by Him to get Nebuchadnezzar's attention; and to teach the people of the Babylonian kingdom to respect the living God.

❧ Chapter 15 ❧

God's Workmanship—
The Man Healed at Siloam

Here is a young man who remains nameless in the Scriptures, but whose story is very important. He is an excellent example of one who waited many years for healing from God, and whose situation was used for the glory of God.

The man had been born blind (John 9:1). When the story recorded in Scripture takes place, he is described by his parents as being "of age" (John 9:21), which means he is at least a young adult. So here is a young adult who was born blind, and up to this point has had no opportunity to live what we might call a normal life. In his society, he had no real way to work a trade or generate income, and so he resorted to sitting in the street asking for handouts from whoever happened to pass by. Today, we have many tools to assist people with physical challenges so that they may pursue an active career, but this man did not have such options. Therefore, he sat and begged.

His situation was very challenging. What hope did he have of enjoying many of the experiences in life that people in his day would have taken for granted? Things like learning a trade, owning a small business, traveling, or getting married were unlikely to occur in his society for one who was born blind.

We, of course, do not know his thoughts, but it is easy to imagine that he had at some point wondered why God had allowed him to be placed in such a situation as this. Why had he been born blind? After all, what could he possibly have done before even being born that would merit such a fate?

His parents probably had questions, too. This situation was, no doubt, extremely challenging for them, as well. One can imagine their concern when, after having a new baby, they learned that something was wrong with his eyes. They must have grieved, they must have prayed, and they must have wondered what brought this on. Was it their fault? Now they would face the extra challenges associated with raising a child who was blind. They likely wondered what God was doing.

The society around them wondered, too.

"... Rabbi, who sinned, this man or his parents, that he was born blind?" (John 9:2) It is evident from this question made by Jesus' disciples as they encountered the man that many concluded either this man or his parents had sinned. His blindness must be somebody's fault in their mind.

Jesus' answer was clear, but it must have shocked His disciples and left them thinking about things.

"... It was not that this man sinned, or his parents, but that the works of God might be displayed in him. We must work the works of him who sent me while it is day; night is coming, when no one can work. As long as I am in the world, I am the light of the world" (John 9:3–5).

I can hear the proponents of the lie of the ages now—*Really? God allowed this man to be born blind, and to wait a couple of decades to be given his sight, all so that He could display His work through him? That seems cruel.*

The problem with this line of thinking is that it assumes, without openly stating it, that being used to display the works of God is no big deal. It assumes that playing a central role in glorifying God is not worth much, and so the grief of being born blind and waiting this long to be healed would (in the minds of some) far outweigh the benefits involved in glorifying God.

Just how big a deal is it to play a central role in glorifying God? We will investigate this very question in more detail in a later chapter, but for now, let's just say that to this unnamed man it seemed very much worth it. We know this by his response to the Pharisees later, as they pressed him hard concerning the identity of his healer.

After making the declaration mentioned above, Jesus healed the man of his blindness.

> Having said these things, he spit on the ground and made mud with the saliva. Then he anointed the man's eyes with the mud, and said to him, "Go, wash in the pool of Siloam" (which means Sent). So he went and washed and came back seeing (John 9:6–7).

The healing of this man caused quite a stir among the people, and so he was brought to the Pharisees. They grilled him with questions as they tried to sort out whether Jesus was of God or not. They thought that if Jesus really were of God, then He would not have been healing on the Sabbath (John 9:16), but this notion came from their traditions and not from God's actual word as recorded in the Scriptures. They pushed the healed man for his answer on the matter.

> So they said again to the blind man, "What do you say about him, since he has opened your eyes?" … (John 9:17).

Here was his chance to speak up. He could have, if he had believed the lie of the ages, complained about having been born blind, questioned what God was doing, and why he had to wait so long to be healed. Instead, he simply said, "He is a prophet" (John 9:17).

In other words, Jesus was from God, and he wondered how it was that those who were the religious leaders could not see that. He saw his help as coming from God, and Jesus as the one whom God had sent to bring it to him.

The leaders of the Jews continued their investigation. They had difficulty believing that the man ever was born blind, and so they questioned his parents about that fact (John 9:18–23). Once this was confirmed, they went back to the man who was healed.

So for a second time, they summoned the man who had been

blind, and said to him, "Give glory to God *[this is what he was about to do, only not in the way that they expected];* we know that this man *[Jesus]* is a sinner." He then answered, "Whether He is a sinner, I do not know; one thing I do know, that though I was blind, now I see."

So they said to him, "What did He do to you? How did He open your eyes?" He answered them, "I told you already and you would not listen; why do you want to hear *it* again? You do not want to become his disciples too, do you?" They spoke abusively to him and said, "You are his disciple, but we are disciples of Moses. We know that God has spoken to Moses, but as for this man, we do not know where he is from." The man answered and said to them, "Well, here is the amazing thing, that you do not know where He is from, and *yet* He opened my eyes! We know that God does not listen to sinners; but if someone is God-fearing and does His will, He listens to him. Since the beginning of time it has never been heard that anyone opened the eyes of a person born blind. If this man were not from God, He could do nothing." They answered him, "You were born entirely in sins *[there goes that false idea again—his blindness was because he had sinned somehow],* and *yet* you are teaching us?" So they put him out (John 9:24–34 NASB).

The phrase "they put him out" does not just mean that they tossed him out of the room, it means he was excommunicated from the temple area (Foster, p. 829). The temple was the center of worship and culture at that time. To be excommunicated was a big deal because this would prevent him from participating in any of the normal privileges of worship in the temple or a synagogue. Privileges which were coming into his reach for the first time in his life were immediately taken away again (Foster, p. 827). He was made an outcast once again.

This man, however, did not become bitter. He had not been bitter about being blind, and now he was not bitter about becoming an outcast. This is evident by what happened next.

Jesus heard that they had put him out, and upon finding him

[that means that Jesus went looking for him], He said, "Do you believe in the Son of Man?" He answered by saying, "And who is He, Sir, that I may believe in Him?" Jesus said to him, "You have both seen Him, and He is the one who is talking with you." And he said, "I believe, Lord." And he worshiped Him (John 9:35–38 NASB).

His actions did not indicate bitterness toward God or toward Jesus. Instead, he stopped and worshiped Jesus. He had been an outcast all his life up to this point, and when he was finally healed and had the chance to become a more normal member of society, he was willing to become an outcast again if that was what it took to stand up for the truth about Jesus. To him, glorifying God was weightier than all that he had suffered by having been blind all that time, and weightier than the blessings of finally being considered a normal member of society. He was willing to put everything on the line to glorify God. I believe that in God's scheme of things, this man remains a true hero.

Chapter 16

God's Workmanship—
The Apostle Paul

The Apostle Paul is one of my favorite persons to read about in all the sacred Scriptures. It would be difficult to read his epistles and miss the passion he has both for the Lord and for His people. Listen as he speaks to the Christians in Corinth.

> Who is weak and I am not weak? Who is made to fall, and I am not indignant? (2 Corinthians 11:29).

And,

> I will most gladly spend and be spent for your souls. If I love you more, am I to be loved less? (2 Corinthians 12:15).

And,

> Make room in your hearts for us. We have wronged no one, we have corrupted no one, we have taken advantage of no one. I do not say this to condemn you, for I said before that you are in our hearts, to die together and to live together (2 Corinthians 7:2–3).

Yet the passion of Paul was not always channeled in a positive direction as far as the church is concerned. When we first meet him in the Bible, he is one who agrees heartily with the execution of Stephen, a Christian. After Stephen is killed, we see him (then known as Saul of Tarsus) leading a passionate persecution of the Lord's church.

> And Saul approved of his execution. And there arose on that

day a great persecution against the church in Jerusalem, and they were all scattered throughout the regions of Judea and Samaria, except the apostles. Devout men buried Stephen and made great lamentation over him. But Saul was ravaging the church, and entering house after house, he dragged off men and women and committed them to prison (Acts 8:1–3).

While he was a Pharisee, he was very passionate about persecuting the church, because he thought at that time that it was a heretical sect. When he had been converted to the truth about Jesus Christ, and became a Christian himself, he became one of the church's most ardent advocates. Whatever he was going to do, he was going to be all in and go all out. There was no halfheartedness to be found in Paul.

What was it that caused an all-out high-ranking Jewish Pharisee to become an all-out Christian and Apostle of Jesus Christ? The answer is simple. He learned that there is no one like Jesus. While he was on his way from Jerusalem to Damascus to find and arrest Christians, he met Jesus.

But Saul, still breathing threats and murder against the disciples of the Lord, went to the high priest and asked him for letters to the synagogues at Damascus, so that if he found any belonging to the Way, men or women, he might bring them bound to Jerusalem. Now as he went on his way, he approached Damascus, and suddenly a light from heaven shone around him. And falling to the ground, he heard a voice saying to him, "Saul, Saul, why are you persecuting me?" And he said, "Who are you, Lord?" And he said, "I am Jesus, whom you are persecuting. But rise and enter the city, and you will be told what you are to do." The men who were traveling with him stood speechless, hearing the voice but seeing no one. Saul rose from the ground, and although his eyes were opened, he saw nothing. So they led him by the hand and brought him into Damascus. And for three days he was without sight, and neither ate nor drank (Acts 9:1–9).

Just meeting Jesus made all the difference in the world. Beforehand, Jesus was to Saul, just a radical and rogue leader of a wayward sect who had been executed by the Romans. Meeting Him in person made all the difference. Now he knew that Jesus was risen from the dead. Now he knew that only the true God could make that happen. Now he knew that it was him who had been wrong and not Jesus or His followers. As Paul wrote in his letter to the Romans, he now knew that this one "was declared to be the Son of God in power according to the Spirit of holiness by his resurrection from the dead, Jesus Christ our Lord" (Romans 1:4).

This man, Saul of Tarsus, was broken and humbled by learning the truth concerning Jesus. The encounter with Jesus on his way to Damascus left him without his eyesight. He was instructed to go to Damascus and wait. A few days later, a man named Ananias, a Christian, was sent to him to proclaim the gospel to him and to heal him of his blindness. How humiliating. He was required to wait and to receive help from one of the very persons that he had started out to find and arrest! Yet he was willing to do it. And Ananias was willing to help him, although he initially had some questions when the Lord told him to go and do it (Acts 9:10–18).

> Then Ananias went to the house and entered it. Placing his hands on Saul, he said, "Brother Saul, the Lord—Jesus, who appeared to you on the road as you were coming here—has sent me so that you may see again and be filled with the Holy Spirit." Immediately, something like scales fell from Saul's eyes, and he could see again. He got up and was baptized, and after taking some food, he regained his strength (Acts 9:17–19 NIV).

Paul's response to this newfound truth about Jesus was immediate and outspoken. We see in the book of Acts that right away he was in the synagogues proclaiming Jesus as the Son of God (Acts 9:20). His testimony concerning Jesus was so effective that those who heard him were both astonished and baffled (Acts 9:21-22). This was so troublesome to the Jews of Damascus that they eventually developed a plot to kill him.

> After many days had gone by, there was a conspiracy among the Jews to kill him, but Saul learned of their plan. Day and night they kept close watch on the city gates in order to kill

him. But his followers took him by night and lowered him in a basket through an opening in the wall (Acts 9:23–25 NIV).

Such was the beginning of Paul's experience as a Christian.

Paul was not only called to be a Christian, but he clearly understood that the Lord had set him apart to be an Apostle of Jesus Christ.

Paul, a servant of Christ Jesus, called to be an apostle, set apart for the gospel of God, which he promised beforehand through his prophets in the holy Scriptures, (Romans 1:1–2).

As an Apostle, he was a leader in the early church, worked special signs that identified him as an Apostle (2 Corinthians 12:12), and received special revelation from God. One of the central points in the first chapter of his letter to the Galatians was that the gospel that he had proclaimed to them was not something that came from himself, and not even something that had been explained to him by other men, but rather came to him by special revelation from God.

For I would have you know, brothers, that the gospel that was preached by me is not man's gospel. For I did not receive it from any man, nor was I taught it, but I received it through a revelation of Jesus Christ. For you have heard of my former life in Judaism, how I persecuted the church of God violently and tried to destroy it. And I was advancing in Judaism beyond many of my own age among my people, so extremely zealous was I for the traditions of my fathers. But when he who had set me apart before I was born, and who called me by his grace, was pleased to reveal his Son to me, in order that I might preach him among the Gentiles, I did not immediately consult with anyone; nor did I go up to Jerusalem to those who were apostles before me, but I went away into Arabia, and returned again to Damascus (Galatians 1:11–17).

The other Apostles recognized this claim, and even confirmed it.

And from those who seemed to be influential (what they were

makes no difference to me; God shows no partiality)—those, I say, who seemed influential added nothing to me. On the contrary, when they saw that I had been entrusted with the gospel to the uncircumcised, just as Peter had been entrusted with the gospel to the circumcised (for he who worked through Peter for his apostolic ministry to the circumcised worked also through me for mine to the Gentiles), and when James and Cephas and John, who seemed to be pillars, perceived the grace that was given to me, they gave the right hand of fellowship to Barnabas and me, that we should go to the Gentiles and they to the circumcised (Galatians 2:6–9).

Paul's faithfulness and zeal for serving the Lord in his calling was unmatched among the other Apostles and early Christians. He completed multiple missionary journeys during which he was instrumental in planting churches throughout Greece, Macedonia, and Asia Minor. He trained and appointed leaders in the churches and visited them regularly. When he could not be present, and problems arose, he wrote epistles to the churches and sent emissaries such as Timothy or Titus, men trained by him for ministry. His epistles count for at least 13 of the 27 books of the New Testament.

Whenever Paul evaluated his own life, he spoke with confidence that he had lived with a clear conscience before God. When explaining the actions of his ministry to the Roman leader Felix, Paul said the following:

But this I confess to you, that according to the Way, which they call a sect, I worship the God of our fathers, believing everything laid down by the Law and written in the Prophets, having a hope in God, which these men themselves accept, that there will be a resurrection of both the just and the unjust. So I always take pains to have a clear conscience toward both God and man (Acts 24:14–16).

To King Agrippa he said of his response to having seen Jesus on the way to Damascus:

Therefore, O King Agrippa, I was not disobedient to the heavenly vision, but declared first to those in Damascus, then in Jerusalem and throughout all the region of Judea, and also to the Gentiles, that they should repent and turn to God, performing deeds in keeping with their repentance (Acts 26:19–20).

To the Corinthians he wrote:

For I am the least of the apostles, unworthy to be called an apostle, because I persecuted the church of God. But by the grace of God I am what I am, and his grace toward me was not in vain. On the contrary, I worked harder than any of them, though it was not I, but the grace of God that is with me (1 Corinthians 15:9–10).

While reflecting on his life and ministry as he wrote his second letter to Timothy, Paul wrote this concerning how he had lived and carried out the ministry to which God had called him:

For I am already being poured out as a drink offering, and the time of my departure has come. I have fought the good fight, I have finished the race, I have kept the faith. Henceforth there is laid up for me the crown of righteousness, which the Lord, the righteous judge, will award to me on that day, and not only to me but also to all who have loved his appearing (2 Timothy 4:6–8).

Obviously, Paul believed, concerning his own life, that he had served God, fulfilled his ministry, and lived well. The other Apostles had apparently agreed. We saw earlier how Peter, James, and John had given Paul the right hand of fellowship and recognized his apostleship to the Gentiles. Peter even referred to him as "our beloved brother Paul," and regarded his epistles as being equal with the other Scriptures (2 Peter 3:15–16).

Yet even though Paul had been zealous and faithful in carrying out his ministry as an Apostle of Jesus Christ, his life was not without episodes of pain and grief. We already saw how, when Paul was first converted and began to preach boldly in Damascus, the Jews there responded by plotting to kill him. Trouble and opposition to his work had presented themselves at the very beginning of his walk with Christ, and later, as he continued serving the Lord, it was no different. Persecution followed him wherever he went. In his second letter to the Christians in Corinth, Paul recounted a list of some of his troubles up to that point. He detailed his experience in this way:

> ... with far greater labors, far more imprisonments, with countless beatings, and often near death. Five times I received at the hands of the Jews the forty lashes less one. Three times I was beaten with rods. Once I was stoned. Three times I was shipwrecked; a night and a day I was adrift at sea; on frequent journeys, in danger from rivers, danger from robbers, danger from my own people, danger from Gentiles, danger in the city, danger in the wilderness, danger at sea, danger from false brothers; in toil and hardship, through many a sleepless night, in hunger and thirst, often without food, in cold and exposure (2 Corinthians 11:23–27).

During all this trouble, Paul did not entertain believing the lie of the ages. He knew that his faithful ministry and hard work did not guarantee him a life free from pain and grief. In fact, in the passage quoted above, he was explaining to the Christians in Corinth that his trials were an evidence to support his claim to be a true Apostle of Jesus Christ, in stark contrast to the false teachers that were troubling them at that time. The false teachers were self-centered and self-serving. They wanted people to follow them; they wanted things to go their way.

Jesus and His true Apostles were selfless. They worked for the benefit of others, even at their own expense. As Jesus had taught earlier during His ministry, the Corinthians could know the true teachers from the false ones by their fruit (Matthew 7:15–20). Paul, therefore, saw his sufferings not as evidence that God had somehow failed him, but rather as a badge of authenticity for his ministry. They served as evidence that he was a true Apostle, and that he was willing to suffer, if need be, to help others and to serve God.

To Paul, experiencing temporary earthly suffering was an insignificant price to pay if that was what was needed to glorify God.

> The Spirit himself bears witness with our spirit that we are children of God, and if children, then heirs—heirs of God and fellow heirs with Christ, provided we suffer with him in order that we may also be glorified with him.
>
> For I consider that the sufferings of this present time are not worth comparing with the glory that is to be revealed to us.
>
> (Romans 8:16–18)

Paul, during the course of his work for the Lord, experienced as much pain and grief as anyone, but he did not lose heart in the midst of his troubles, because he rejected the lie of the ages and kept his focus on what he called an "eternal weight of glory" (2 Corinthians 4:17).

As we saw earlier, he would rather spend and be spent when necessary to be a blessing to others and to glorify God. His unselfish focus on the eternal things kept him from losing heart.

> But we have this treasure in earthen containers, so that the extraordinary *greatness* of the power will be of God and not from ourselves; *we are* afflicted in every way, but not crushed; perplexed, but not despairing; persecuted, but not abandoned; struck down, but not destroyed; always carrying around in the body the dying of Jesus, so that the life of Jesus also may be revealed in our body. For we who live are constantly being handed over to death because of Jesus, so that the life of Jesus also may be revealed in our mortal flesh. So death works in us, but life in you.
>
> But having the same spirit of faith, according to what is written, "I BELIEVED, THEREFORE I SPOKE," we also believe, therefore we also speak, knowing that He who raised the Lord Jesus will also raise us with Jesus, and will present *us* with you. For all things *are* for your sakes, so that the grace, having spread to more and more people, will cause thanksgiving to overflow to the glory of God.
>
> Therefore we do not lose heart, but though our outer person is decaying, yet our inner *person* is being renewed day by day.

For our momentary, light affliction is producing for us an eternal weight of glory far beyond all comparison, while we look not at the things which are seen, but at the things which are not seen; for the things which are seen are temporal, but the things which are not seen are eternal.

(2 Corinthians 4:7–18 NASB)

If God had not brought Paul through such difficulty, pain, and grief as He did, these words might seem trite to those experiencing suffering. But when one knows who Paul is and what the Lord brought him through, the words carry weight. Paul saw his trouble as an opportunity for God to be glorified.

Chapter 17

An Eternal Weight of Glory

I suspect that many of us today do not fully comprehend the weight of what it means to glorify God. The Apostle Paul claimed that his "light and momentary affliction" was producing an "eternal weight of glory beyond all comparison" (2 Corinthians 4:17). His afflictions do not seem momentary or light to me. Maybe that is because I cannot yet see the weight of glory he is talking about.

In mathematics it is said that one can determine the value of an unknown variable in an equation if one has enough information about the other terms in the equation. For example, let's say that we have the equation a times b equals c. If we know the value of c and the value of b, then we can easily determine the value of a. I believe it is like that with the theological topic that we are addressing here, as well. We know that God is good, we know that He has demonstrated by His actions that He loves each one of us (Romans 5:6–10), and we know that He is willing to allow people to suffer for a time if it means that He will be glorified (i.e. Mary, Martha, Lazarus, and the many other examples throughout the Scriptures); therefore, we can conclude that glorifying Him is worth the pain and must be something very good for us as well as for Him; the weight of this glory must be highly significant, even if we cannot yet fully measure it. This is exactly why the Apostle Paul said, "For I consider that the sufferings of this present time are not worth comparing with the glory that is to be revealed to us" (Romans 8:18).

Every parent knows that there are times when one must take their child through a moment of temporary and brief pain in order to bring them to a far greater good. We know of examples like cleansing a wound, or getting a vaccination, or taking some nasty-tasting medicine to be healed from an illness. A moment of discomfort is far outweighed by the significance of the good it brings.

Jesus talked about this concept. He described the situation in which a woman is about to give birth:

> When a woman is giving birth, she has sorrow because her hour has come, but when she has delivered the baby, she no longer remembers the anguish, for joy that a human being has been born into the world (John 16:21).

The pain associated with the delivery does not seem light at the time of delivery. Even so, while typically the pain lasts several hours, the blessing of the new life being born lasts a lifetime and beyond. The weight of the blessing far surpasses the weight of the affliction. In the passage above, Jesus used this illustration to explain to His disciples what things were soon going to be like for them. He was about to face arrest, ridicule, suffering, and death. Yet all this would be eclipsed shortly afterward by His resurrection from the dead, and then the gift of eternal life He was planning to give them.

The concept is the same for us today. As we follow Christ, serve God, and live life for Him, persecution will come; sometimes pain will come; sometimes illness will come; and eventually (unless the Lord returns first), physical death will come. No one lives life without experiencing tribulation and grief (John 16:33). Even so, if we serve God and seek His glory in everything, even in the tribulation, then the weight of the blessing is immeasurably greater.

In the fifteenth chapter of his letter to the Romans, Paul writes of the importance of sacrificing in order to glorify God:

> Now may the God who gives perseverance and encouragement grant you to be of the same mind with one another, according to Christ Jesus, so that with one purpose *and* one voice you may glorify the God and Father of our Lord Jesus Christ.

> Therefore, accept one another, just as Christ also accepted us, for the glory of God. For I say that Christ has become a servant to the circumcision in behalf of the truth of God, to confirm the promises *given* to the fathers, and for the Gentiles to glorify God for His mercy; … (Romans 15:5–9 NASB).

The extent to which we believe in the eternal weight of God's glory will drive our responses as we face life and its painful issues. The question is how important is it, really, to glorify God? How much weight does it carry in one's mind and heart? Many today seem to give it little thought.

For Jesus, however, His every thought, His every breath, His every word, His every movement, and His every action were for the specific purpose of glorifying His Father. He made no exception, ever.

So Jesus said to them, "Truly, truly, I say to you, the Son can do nothing of his own accord, but only what he sees the Father doing. For whatever the Father does, that the Son does likewise" (John 5:19).

And,

"I can do nothing on my own. As I hear, I judge, and my judgment is just, because I seek not my own will but the will of him who sent me" (John 5:30).

While praying to His Father near the end of His earthly ministry, He said, "I glorified you on earth, having accomplished the work that you gave me to do" (John 17:4). He lived and He died for the glory of His Father—period. It was that important to Him.

Consider the prophets of old. They preferred to experience pain, grief, and even death, rather than live a life that did not glorify God. Jeremiah could not help but speak the words that God had caused to burn in his bones (Jeremiah 20:9). Ezekiel, for part of his life, was mute unless he was specifically prophesying for the Lord (Ezekiel 3:25–27). Isaiah was told to walk naked and barefoot for a time to illustrate an important point to his hearers (Isaiah 20:1–6). Daniel would rather be thrown into a den of lions than not pray to God (Daniel 6:1–28). All of these, and more, understood that glorifying God was immeasurably weightier than any difficulty they might have been asked to face.

Recently, as I was reflecting on this, I felt convicted by the wholehearted dedication of these servants of God. I began to realize that in my own life experience I had not been giving anything like enough thought to answering the question, "How much weight does glorifying God carry in my daily life decisions, both large and small? How much am I willing to suffer, really, if that is what it takes to glorify God?" Though I am doing better with this now, I still have much to learn.

The contemporary Christian band MercyMe recorded a song entitled "Bring the Rain," which expresses the importance of being willing to walk through difficult times if that is what it takes to glorify God. Here are the lyrics (used by permission):

> I can count a million times
>
> People asking me how I
>
> Can praise You with all that I've gone through
>
> The question just amazes me
>
> Can circumstances possibly
>
> Change who I forever am in You
>
> Maybe since my life was changed
>
> Long before these rainy days
>
> It's never really crossed my mind
>
> To turn my back on you, oh Lord
>
> My only shelter from the storm
>
> But instead I draw closer through these times
>
> So I pray
>
> Bring me joy, bring me peace
>
> Bring the chance to be free
>
> Bring me anything that brings You glory
>
> And I know there'll be days
>
> When this life brings me pain
>
> But if that's what it takes to praise You
>
> Jesus, bring the rain

I am yours regardless of

The dark clouds that may loom above

Because You are much greater than my pain

You who made a way for me

By suffering Your destiny

So tell me, what's a little rain

So I pray

Holy, holy, holy

Is the Lord God Almighty (MercyMe, "Bring the Rain")

Not only is glorifying God something that has tremendous weight, but it is also something that is extremely long lasting. Paul did not mention a brief weight of glory as he wrote to the Corinthians, but an *eternal* weight of glory. Is it asking too much to suffer something for a moment in time in order to receive a blessing that is both weighty and unending? The blessing does not end— ever. Sometimes, we want to settle for temporary earthly pleasure and comfort, when what we could have instead is an eternal weight of glory.

C. S. Lewis put it this way:

Indeed, if we consider the unblushing promises of reward and the staggering nature of the rewards promised in the Gospels, it would seem that Our Lord finds our desires not too strong, but too weak. We are half-hearted creatures, fooling about with drink and sex and ambition when infinite joy is offered us, like an ignorant child who wants to go on making mud pies in a slum because he cannot imagine what is meant by an offer of a holiday at the sea. We are far too easily pleased (Lewis, *The Weight of Glory*, pp. 3–4).

What God offers to each one of us is not chintzy. It is weighty and it is eternal. It is no less than an infinite and intimate relationship with Himself. What He is seeking in all of this is a healthy relationship with each person He created.

God wants you to know Him, and He wants you to experience the blessedness of an intensely rich fellowship with Him forever. If He should take you through some pain and some grief to get you there, just know that His intentions are to bless you beyond what you could ever measure right now.

> Now to him who is able to do far more abundantly than all that we ask or think, according to the power at work within us, to him be glory in the church and in Christ Jesus throughout all generations, forever and ever. Amen (Ephesians 3:20–21).

Chapter 18

Jesus' Friends—Perplexed Once Again

We saw in the early chapters of this book that Jesus led His friends Mary, Martha, and Lazarus down a path in which their pain and their grief was temporarily increased so that they could be included in an important plan that glorified God. They were, nevertheless, soon delivered from their grief by the raising of Lazarus from the dead. What we did not mention at that time was that, just a few weeks later, the Lord led them down a similar path once again. This time, however, the one to enter suffering, pain, and eventually, death was not Lazarus, but Jesus Himself. Jesus, their beloved friend, who understood their pain; who grieved with them; and who then brought their brother back to life was soon arrested, falsely accused, ridiculed in public, beaten, scourged, and then put to death through cruel Roman crucifixion.

Imagine the grief of Mary, Martha, and Lazarus as they witnessed these things take place. They must have wondered, "How can this be? How can God allow One so noble and so powerful to be treated this way? The One whom we know to be the long-awaited Messiah?" They must have been hurt and perplexed.

The arrest, the suffering, and the death of Jesus made little sense to any of His friends and followers at the time these things took place. His friend, Judas, betrayed Him; most of His disciples fled when He was arrested; Peter denied that he ever knew Him; and they were hiding in fear from the Jewish leaders after His death. At the time Jesus died, few people seemed to believe that He would still come into His kingdom and take His proper throne—except one of the thieves that was crucified next to Him (Luke 23:40–43).

So why did God allow all this to happen to His own Son? Why did Jesus suffer, and why did He die? We often hear Christians and people who hang around Christians say that Jesus died for our sins. But what does that mean? Why did He die, why was it necessary that He die to save people from their sins, and how does His dying accomplish this? The answer to these questions will be our focus at this time.

The Authority of God, the Creator

The first point in understanding why Jesus suffered and died is to know that God is the Creator, and to understand what authority goes along with that position. The Bible teaches that God created the heavens and the earth (Genesis 1:1), and all they contain (John 1:1–3). At first glance, you might wonder what this has to do with why Jesus suffered and died, but as we shall see, this basic fact is foundational to comprehending the redemptive work of the Son of God.

God's Word makes no explanation for why everything exists, outside of the clear statement that God created all things visible, all things invisible, and that He sustains all created things by the word of His power.

All things were made through him, and without him was not any thing made that was made (John 1:3).

Long ago, at many times and in many ways, God spoke to our fathers by the prophets, but in these last days he has spoken to us by his Son, whom he appointed the heir of all things, through whom also he created the world. He is the radiance of the glory of God and the exact imprint of his nature, and he upholds the universe by the word of his power … (Hebrews 1:1–3).

By faith we understand that the universe was created by the word of God, so that what is seen was not made out of things that are visible (Hebrews 11:3).

In the sacred Scriptures we see that the fact of creation forms a basis for the worship of God, the Creator.

"Worthy are you, our Lord and God, to receive glory and honor and power, for you created all things, and by your will they existed and were created (Revelation 4:11).

Give thanks to the God of gods,
    for his steadfast love endures forever.
Give thanks to the Lord of lords,
    for his steadfast love endures forever;
to him who alone does great wonders,
    for his steadfast love endures forever;
to him who by understanding made the heavens,
    for his steadfast love endures forever;
to him who spread out the earth above the waters,
    for his steadfast love endures forever; (Psalm 136:2–6).

So, because God has created all things, including man, man gives thanks and worships Him. Romans Chapter 1 teaches us that man owes worship and thanksgiving to God as Creator and is without excuse if it is not offered.

As the author of all creation, God has ownership and authority over it. This concept is both logical and biblical. The words author and authority share the same root. The Scriptures teach that since God is the Creator, He is also the owner or possessor of that which He has created.

The earth is the LORD's and the fullness thereof,
    the world and those who dwell therein,
for he has founded it upon the seas
    and established it upon the rivers (Psalm 24:1–2).

Know that the LORD, he is God!
    It is he who made us, and we are his;
    we are his people, and the sheep of his pasture.
                                    (Psalm 100:3)

We humans generally understand this logic. If an artist paints a painting, it is considered to be their painting, and if an inventor invents something, it is considered to be their invention. In the same way, since God created the heavens, the earth, all things visible, and all things invisible, they are His creation.

As the author of His creation, God, the Creator, has the authority to define right and wrong behavior for his creatures, to command obedience, and to punish disobedience. No one else has the authority to define sin, since no one else has created the world and no one else is the owner of the creation in the same way that God is. Contrary to the opinion of many people in our time, man does not have the authority to define what is right and wrong behavior. This is the unique domain of God, the Creator.

Dr. Jack Cottrell explains:

True and absolute ethical obligation is grounded in the fact that God is our Creator. When God says, "Listen to My voice" (Jeremiah 11:7), why should we listen? When Jesus says, "Keep My commandments" (John 14:15), why should we? "You should diligently keep the commandments of the Lord your God, and His testimonies and His statutes which He has commanded you" (Deuteronomy 6:17). Who says? Well, *God* says, and he just happens to be the Creator. Being Creator gives God the rights of ownership: "The earth is the Lord's, and all it contains, the world, and those who dwell in it. For He has founded it upon the seas, and established it upon the rivers" (Psalm 24:1–2). God as Creator (and therefore owner) has the absolute right to lay down the rules for his creation (Cottrell, *Creator*, pp. 163–164).

The founding fathers of the United States of America recognized this concept, and went so far as to write it into the nation's founding document, the Declaration of Independence. It says:

We hold these truths to be self-evident, that all Men are created equal, that they are endowed by their Creator with certain unalienable Rights, that among these are Life, Liberty, and the Pursuit of Happiness—That to secure these Rights, Governments are instituted among Men, deriving their just powers from the Consent of the Governed, ... (Sterling, 2012 edition, p. 81).

To the founding fathers of the United States, the truth that God is Creator, and therefore, the One who defines which unalienable rights the civil government ought to secure, was a truth so obvious that they called it "self-evident."

Another thing that people have no right to do is make up their own idea of who or what they think God is. Many people think that whatever you believe about God is okay, if you are sincere. I am not sure what is meant by sincere in this case, but I have often heard people talk this way. The problem is that when things are real, you cannot just make up whatever you want about how they are and how they work. You can sincerely believe that a thing is so and yet be wrong. I have heard that there was a time when some people thought that the moon was made of cheese because of the apparent texture of its surface when viewed from earth. Yet when the Apollo astronauts landed on it, they found it to be made of rock and dust—so back when some people sincerely believed it to be made of cheese, it was really rock and dust the whole time. When something is real, its nature must be discovered through investigation and research. In the same way, if God is real, you cannot just make up your own ideas about what He is like, you must do the research in His Word and discover what He has told us about Himself.

The Apostle Paul touched on this point when he came to Athens to proclaim God's good news in that location. The book of Acts records his words and actions while he was there.

Now while Paul was waiting for them at Athens, his spirit was provoked within him as he saw that the city was full of idols (Acts 17:16).

So Paul stood in the midst of the Areopagus and said, "Men of Athens, I see that you are very religious in all respects. For while I was passing through and examining the objects of your worship, I also found an altar with this inscription, 'TO AN UNKNOWN GOD.' Therefore what you worship in ignorance, this I proclaim to you. The God who made the world and everything that is in it, since He is Lord of heaven and earth, does not dwell in temples made by hands; nor is He served by human hands, as though He needed anything, since He Himself gives to all *people* life and breath and all things, and He made from one *man* every nation of mankind to live on all the face of the earth, having determined *their* appointed times and the boundaries of their habitation, that they would seek God, if perhaps they might feel around for Him and find *Him*, though He is not far from each one of us; for in Him we live and move and exist, as even some of your own poets have said, 'For we also are His descendants.' Therefore, since we are the descendants of God, we ought not to think that the Divine *Nature* is like gold or silver or stone, an image formed by human skill and thought. So having overlooked the times of ignorance, God is now proclaiming to mankind that all people everywhere are to repent, because He has set a day on which He will judge the world in righteousness through a Man whom He has appointed, having furnished proof to all people by raising Him from the dead" (Acts 17:22–31 NASB).

The main ideas here seem to be that God has created all things and causes them to exist; since He is Creator, we must not think He is formed by human skill and thought. We must let Him define Himself. Furthermore, one central thing that God has to say about all people everywhere is that they need to repent (i.e., stop disobeying Him). Therefore, it is **His** Word that defines morality and not the popular opinion of culture.

All people have an obligation to let God define Himself and a moral obligation to obey Him as their Creator and sovereign Lord. The problem comes in when people do not obey their Creator.

God Responds with Justice

How does God respond when people, whom He created in His image (Genesis 1:26–27), choose to disobey Him and to break His commandments? The answer, as found in the Bible, is twofold.

The answer is twofold because God's nature consists of two dominant aspects. One must understand that when thinking about and responding to God, the Creator, one is dealing with perfection. He is perfect holiness (involving justice) and He is perfect love (involving grace and mercy). God responds to the disobedience of humans in relation to both aspects of His own nature. Dr. Cottrell comments,

> When righteousness is properly understood as a distinct attribute in its own right, we are able to get a better perspective on love and holiness as equally fundamental sides of the nature of God "who is able to save and destroy" (James 4:12). Paul reflects both aspects of God in Romans 11:22. "Behold then the kindness and severity of God." While each is tempered by the other, each may be expressed independently of the other (Cottrell, *Redeemer*, p. 256).

God's actions and words are always completely consistent with His own nature. No one outside of Himself makes Him do this, He makes Himself do it. There exists no authority outside of Himself to which He is accountable (Hebrews 6:13), yet in His own nature He requires it of Himself to always be consistent. Consider these statements from the Apostle Paul:

> if we are faithless, he remains faithful—for he cannot deny himself (2 Timothy 2:13).

And,

> in the hope of eternal life, which God, who cannot lie, promised long ages ago, (Titus 1:2 NASB).

I believe the reason that God cannot lie is because He cannot disown Himself, as stated by Paul in 2 Timothy, Chapter 2. He cannot and will not ever choose to do anything that is contrary to His own nature. He is no hypocrite. He is consistent and He does not change (Hebrews 13:8). Since God is perfectly consistent, His word can never be false. His word is always true because He is always true. Jesus stated thus, and it is recorded for us in the tenth chapter of John.

Jesus answered them, "Is it not written in your Law, 'I said, you are gods'? If he called them gods to whom the word of God came—**and Scripture cannot be broken**—do you say of him whom the Father consecrated and sent into the world, 'You are blaspheming,' because I said, 'I am the Son of God'? (John 10:34-36—emphasis added).

Jesus is here defending His right to call himself the Son of God, and in the process of doing so, He quotes one of the Psalms, calls it Scripture, and says that it cannot be broken. What does this mean, that it cannot be broken? Once, I was studying this particular passage with one of my daughters, who was about fifteen years old at the time, and I asked her this very question. She said, "Well, when something is broken, then it doesn't work. So, that means that God's Word cannot ever not work." I was flabbergasted with the wisdom of my fifteen-year-old daughter. That's it! God's Word cannot ever "not work." It always works. It is always true. This is because He is perfect, and He cannot lie.

Therefore, His commandments given to His creatures cannot be broken without consequence. When a person, made in God's image, breaks one of His commandments, it is a violation of justice. This justice is not arbitrary, rather it comes forth from the very nature of God Himself. His laws and commandments are reflections of His nature. He says, "You shall not lie," because He is truthful and consistent. He says, "You shall not commit adultery," because He is faithful and loving. He says, "You shall not commit murder," because He is the life-giver, and the only One who has complete authority to decide when and how life is to be given and taken. And so it goes. To disobey Him and to break His commandments is to commit an affront to His authority, and to insult who He is as a person. It is not only a legal and a moral violation of His law, but also a personal offense against Him.

Because of this, the Bible teaches that God responds to the sin of mankind with perfect justice which includes His personal wrath. People do not like to think about God as having wrath, but the Bible teaches it is so.

For the wrath of God is revealed from heaven against all

ungodliness and unrighteousness of men, who by their unrighteousness suppress the truth (Romans 1:18).

God, in His holiness, responds to the sin of mankind with perfect righteous judgment, according to His Word. Romans, Chapter 2 does a good job of explaining how this works.

Perfect Judgment According to God's Law

Most people today probably do not stop to think very long about what judgment according to law will be like, in an absolutely perfect court of law, before an absolutely perfect, completely righteous, and eternally sovereign judge. We humans tend to cut each other a lot of slack because all of us have a measure of corruption (Romans 3:23). God, the Creator, has none. He is perfect and His Word is perfect. Every single tenet of His perfect Word will be fulfilled without exception. As we saw above, Jesus affirmed that God's Word is truth, it cannot be broken, and not one pen stroke of it will ever pass away until all is fulfilled and accomplished (Matthew 5:17–18). This certainly applies to the judgment of sin.

Perfect judgment works like this: the one who breaks a commandment pays the penalty. This is without exception. Here is how the Apostle Paul explains it:

> He will render to each one according to his works: to those who by patience in well-doing seek for glory and honor and immortality, he will give eternal life; but for those who are self-seeking and do not obey the truth, but obey unrighteousness, there will be wrath and fury. There will be tribulation and distress for every human being who does evil, the Jew first and also the Greek, but glory and honor and peace for everyone who does good, the Jew first and also the Greek. For God shows no partiality (Romans 2:6–11).

So there it is. By judgment under God's law, the one who persists in doing good and who obeys God will be given honor and eternal life, but the one who is self-seeking, disobedient to God, and who does evil will be punished. There are no exceptions, and there is no partiality. According to the passage above, the punishment for doing evil will include wrath, fury, tribulation, and distress. By judgment according to law, all you must do to receive honor and eternal life is commit no sin. If this law is perfect, and the judge is perfect, then you must be perfect to be given eternal life in this way. The problem is that all people have sinned. Paul states that no one can be justified before God in this way because all have committed at least some sins:

> Now we know that whatever the law says it speaks to those who are under the law, so that every mouth may be stopped, and the whole world may be held accountable to God. For by the works of the law no human being will be justified in his sight, since through the law comes knowledge of sin (Romans 3:19–20).

And,

> for all have sinned and fall short of the glory of God, (Romans 3:23).

Here is another passage about judgment:

> Then I saw a great white throne and him who was seated on it. From his presence earth and sky fled away, and no place was found for them. And I saw the dead, great and small, standing before the throne, and books were opened. Then another book was opened, which is the book of life. And the dead were judged by what was written in the books, according to what they had done. And the sea gave up the dead who were in it, Death and Hades gave up the dead who were in them, and they were judged, each one of them, according to what they had done. Then Death and Hades were thrown into the lake of fire. This is the second death, the lake of fire. And if anyone's name was not found written in the book of life, he was thrown into the lake of fire (Revelation 20:11–15).

It says here that there is a record of what each one has done (books were opened), and they are judged, each one, according to that record. We need to understand that God is omniscient, He has all the data. He lacks no information concerning each one of us, and how we have lived our lives. He knows what we have done, he knows what we have said, and He knows exactly why we did and said these things. No data is missing, and He misunderstands nothing. The Scriptures teach that, during the judgment, God will take into account the deeds one does with one's body (2 Corinthians 5:10), the words one has spoken with the one's mouth (Matthew 12:36), and the thoughts and intentions of the heart that motivated these deeds and words (Jeremiah 17:10 and Revelation 2:23).

So, no information is missing, and none of the information is misinterpreted. No one can say to the Lord as they are judged, "But, but, You don't understand!" He does understand. There is no excuse for the wrong that each one of us has done. Judgment, according to law before a perfect God, will take every bit of information into account, and will do it perfectly. Thus, Paul writes, "… the Scripture has confined everyone under sin, …" (Galatians 3:22 NASB).

And, as we saw earlier,

Now we know that whatever the law says it speaks to those who are under the law, so that every mouth may be stopped, and the whole world may be held accountable to God (Romans 3:19).

Therefore, each one of us who has sinned, and that is all of us, needs a rescue from the just penalty for our sins.

God Responds with Love

It was mentioned earlier in this chapter that there are two primary aspects to God's nature—His perfect holiness and His perfect love. We have just explained what the Scriptures describe concerning how His perfect holiness (involving justice) responds to the sin of mankind. We must now also consider how His perfect love (involving mercy and grace) responds to the sin of mankind.

Earlier we saw that God cannot deny His own nature. He cannot be untrue to Himself. This applies to His love as well as to His justice. His love is perfect and endures forever. Psalm 136 repeats 26 times that God's "steadfast love endures forever." The Apostle John wrote these words concerning the love of God:

> Beloved, let us love one another, for love is from God, and whoever loves has been born of God and knows God. Anyone who does not love does not know God, because God is love (1 John 4:7–8).

Obviously, love is a core aspect of the nature of God.

So, how does the love of God respond to the sin of mankind? John goes on to tell us:

> In this the love of God was made manifest among us, that God sent His only Son into the world, so that we might live through him. In this is love, not that we have loved God but that he loved us and sent his Son to be the propitiation for our sins (1 John 4:9–10).

God's perfect justice responds to each person's sin by pronouncing the just penalty for that sin, but God's perfect love responds to each person's sin with an active effort to forgive and rescue that same person from the due penalty. This is why God sent His only begotten Son into the world. Many people are familiar with John 3:16:

> "For God so loved the world, that he gave his only Son, that whoever believes in him should not perish but have eternal life. For God did not send his Son into the world to condemn the world, but in order that the world might be saved through him" (John 3:16–17).

This passage says that "the world" is saved through Him, but how does that work? This is best explained by the Apostles themselves. Paul, for example, wrote this:

> For our sake he [God, the Father] made him [Jesus, the Son] to be sin who knew no sin, so that in him we might become

the righteousness of God (2 Corinthians 5:21).

The first point to understand from this passage is that Jesus knew no sin. Though He is fully human and has fully experienced temptation as a human, nevertheless, He has committed no sin, ever. He kept all His Father's commandments.

> Since then we have a great high priest who has passed through the heavens, Jesus, the Son of God, let us hold fast our confession. For we do not have a high priest who is unable to sympathize with our weaknesses, but one who in every respect has been tempted as we are, yet without sin (Hebrews 4:14–15).

Having never sinned, Jesus fulfilled all the requirements of God's law in terms of keeping His commandments or statutes.

The second point to understand from the 2 Corinthians 5:21 passage is that God, the Father, made Jesus, the Son, "to be sin" so that each one of us (those who have sinned) could become the "righteousness of God" in Him. What this means is that Jesus was willing to trade places with those who had sinned.

Earlier in this chapter it was pointed out how all people (except Jesus) have sinned and fall short of measuring up to God's glory. God's Word teaches that the penalty for having sinned is death.

> The LORD God took the man and put him in the garden of Eden to work it and keep it. And the LORD God commanded the man, saying, "You may surely eat of every tree of the garden, but of the tree of the knowledge of good and evil you shall not eat, for in the day that you eat of it you shall surely die" (Genesis 2:15–17).

> Behold, all souls are mine; the soul of the father as well as the soul of the son is mine: the soul who sins shall die (Ezekiel 18:4).

> For the wages of sin is death, but the free gift of God is eternal life in Christ Jesus our Lord (Romans 6:23).

Jesus, who committed no sin, was willing to step forward and take the penalty that He did not owe in place of those who did owe it. In so doing, He not only fulfills the requirements of God's law regarding the keeping of the commandments, but also fulfills the requirements of God's law in terms paying the penalty (Romans 8:4). God's law consists of His commandments, and of the penalties for breaking them (Cottrell, *Redeemer*, pp. 263–264), and Jesus fulfills all aspects of both—the result being that He can now offer forgiveness to those who have broken God's law.

When Jesus suffered and died, it was no accident. Things did not just get out of hand. Rather, as Peter put it, it was according to the "predetermined plan and foreknowledge of God" (Acts 2:23 NASB). God was in Christ reconciling the world to Himself (2 Corinthians 5:19).

The perfect love of God was responding to the sin of mankind. He was making a way to fulfill all His Word and all His law, and yet still offer to each person a way to receive forgiveness even though they had sinned. God remained true to His own justice and remained true to His own love. Paul sums it up this way:

> But now the righteousness of God has been manifested apart from the law, although the Law and the Prophets bear witness to it—the righteousness of God through faith in Jesus Christ for all who believe. For there is no distinction: for all have sinned and fall short of the glory of God, and are justified by his grace as a gift, through the redemption that is in Christ Jesus, whom God put forward as a propitiation by his blood, to be received by faith. This was to show God's righteousness, because in his divine forbearance he had passed over former sins. It was to show his righteousness at the present time, so that he might be just and the justifier of the one who has faith in Jesus (Romans 3:21–26).

That is why Jesus was willing to suffer and die. He is no fool. Because of the joy that was set before Him (saving His people forever), He endured the cross, despising its suffering and its shame (Hebrews 12:2). Doing so was the only way that God would remain just, and yet be the justifier of people who had sinned. Now they can be offered real forgiveness without God's Word or nature being violated. Jesus' love for the Father and His love for each individual person is why He was willing to suffer and to die. As always, He had our best interests at heart.

Even though Mary, Martha, and Lazarus went through this intensely painful time as Jesus, their dear friend and hero, was brutally tortured and killed, we shall see in the next chapter that it wasn't long before they learned that He was to overcome death once again with glorious power.

Chapter 19

He Restored Their Fortunes Yet Again

In my studies through God's Word, I have come to believe that when the Lord allows one of His children to suffer loss, He will always restore their fortune, and will do it in such a way that their latter blessing is even greater than the original. As we have seen in the examples shown throughout this book, the child of God may be required to wait, sometimes even until the arrival of the new heavens and the new earth, but the lost blessing will always be restored.

When Mary, Martha, and Lazarus experienced the terrible loss of their dear friend and Lord Jesus, they were no exception. It wasn't very long before Jesus presented Himself alive to several of His disciples with convincing evidence (Acts 1:3).

There is no question that their loss was great. Jesus would stay in their house and they could talk with Him; listen to Him; share a meal together; and give Him a hug. Yet all of that was lost when He was arrested; put to death; and sealed up in a cold stone tomb. Their ability to fellowship with Him was taken away. He was dead. The weight of their loss and grief is something we cannot measure.

Imagine their delight, however, when news of His resurrection began to work its way back to them.

The women who had come with him from Galilee followed and saw the tomb and how his body was laid. Then they returned and prepared spices and ointments.

On the Sabbath they rested according to the commandment. But on the first day of the week, at early dawn, they went to the tomb, taking the spices they had prepared. And they found the stone rolled away from the tomb, but when they went in they did not find the body of the Lord Jesus. While they were perplexed about this, behold, two men stood by them in dazzling apparel. And as they were frightened and bowed their faces to the ground, the men said to them, "Why do you seek the living among the dead? He is not here, but has risen. Remember how he told you, while he was still in Galilee, that the Son of Man must be delivered into the hands of sinful men and be crucified and on the third day rise." And they remembered his words, and returning from the tomb they told all these things to the eleven and to all the rest. Now it was Mary Magdalene and Joanna and Mary the mother of James and the other women with them who told these things to the apostles, (Luke 23:55–24:10).

R. C. Foster suggests that at least some of the women that went to the tomb on that resurrection day probably came from Mary and Martha's house in Bethany (Foster, p. 1331). It is possible, and not at all unlikely, that one or both were in this group of women. But even if they were not, it would not have taken long for the word of His resurrection and appearances to get back to them. They must have squealed with delight as they thought something like, *What?! The Master is alive? What does all of this mean?*

Jesus Shattered Expectations

After Jesus' ministry became well known, people began to expect that He could heal sick people, but if someone had already died, most did not expect that He could still do something about it. A classic case in point was when a fellow named Jairus, who was a ruler of one of the synagogues, had a daughter who became very ill. Mark, Chapter 5 has the account. Jairus went and found Jesus, asked Him to come and heal his daughter. Jesus was willing, and began to go with him to where his daughter was, but on the way they were interrupted by a woman who also needed healing. During the delay, Jairus' daughter died. People came from Jairus' home and said, "Your daughter is dead. Why trouble the Teacher any further?" (Mark 5:35). In other words, they expected Jesus could do something for the daughter if she were still alive, but once she died their idea was that then it was too late. Nothing more could have been done at that point. She was dead. Jesus could have dealt with the sickness, but do not expect Him to be able to deal with death itself.

Jesus shattered their expectations and raised her from dead (Mark 5:36–43), demonstrating that He could not only deal with sickness, but He could certainly deal with death, as well.

As we have already seen, a similar thing happened with Martha, Mary, and their brother, Lazarus. The people thought He could help if Lazarus were still alive, but once he died, well, who can deal with that? Jesus shattered their expectations.

He also raised a young man from the dead in a town called Nain (Luke 7:11–17). He was the only son of a widow. Jesus surprised them all by walking up to the funeral procession and raising the young man from the dead. No need for the funeral after that!

After all these things happened, it is reasonable to assume that people began to adjust their expectations a bit: *Okay, so He can raise the dead, we get it, but now He is dead Himself. Who can do anything about that? Who is going to raise Jesus Himself?*

The Chief Priests and Jewish leaders certainly did not think anyone could. To them, despite Jesus having raised Lazarus, death was still the most powerful weapon they had for stopping the young Rabbi and His followers. In fact, they were even plotting to kill Lazarus again, as well, to stop people from believing in Jesus (John 12:9–11). They expected that death was the final and most powerful answer to what they perceived to be their problem.

Jesus had news for them. He shattered their expectations again, this time with His own resurrection. He was crucified, wrapped in cloth and spices, placed in a tomb, and the tomb sealed and guarded by soldiers. Three days of silence passed. Then, wham! There are angels appearing, a great stone moved away, soldiers passed out on the ground and then later running away, an empty tomb, and the Lord appearing alive to several of His followers. The God who breathed life into a pile of dust and made Adam become a living soul is certainly capable of giving life to a dead body. He is the author of life.

What the Resurrection Means

When Jesus was speaking to Martha just before He raised Lazarus from the dead, He said, "I am the resurrection and the life. Whoever believes in me, though he die, yet shall he live," (John 11:25). He also said to His disciples, "Because I live, you also will live" (John 14:19). Jesus is the source of our life, and He promises eternal life to all who believe in Him. If He, Himself, were dead, how could He deliver on that promise?

What if you won a sweepstakes in which the prize was a new home, and then when you went to claim the prize, you found out that the company running the sweepstakes did not actually possess the home? They cannot give you what they do not possess. The whole thing would be a cheat and a fraud. When Jesus promises eternal life to those who believe in Him, we know He can make good on that promise because He has demonstrated by His resurrection that He has power over life and death.

The Apostles frequently taught that Jesus' resurrection is central to the Christian faith. Paul, for example, wrote:

And if Christ has not been raised, your faith is futile and you are still in your sins. Then those also who have fallen asleep in Christ have perished. If in Christ we have hope in this life only, we are of all people most to be pitied.

But in fact Christ has been raised from the dead, the firstfruits of those who have fallen asleep. For as by a man came death, by a man has come also the resurrection of the dead. For as in Adam all die, so also in Christ shall all be made alive (1 Corinthians 15:17–22).

Jesus' resurrection from the dead is actual physical proof that He can make good on His promise to impart life to those who trust in Him. It is the ultimate miracle, and the ultimate demonstration of power.

The resurrection also serves as a declaration as to who Jesus is. The charge for which He was condemned to death by the Jewish leaders was blasphemy. The reason they charged Him with blasphemy was because He claimed to be the Son of God.

> … Again the high priest asked him, "Are you the Christ, the Son of the Blessed?" And Jesus said, "I am, and you will see the Son of Man seated at the right hand of Power, and coming with the clouds of heaven." And the high priest tore his garments and said, "What further witnesses do we need? You have heard his blasphemy. What is your decision?" And they all condemned him as deserving death (Mark 14:61–64).

Well, I can think of a reason to have further witnesses. How about this—to find out if His claim to be the Son of God is true? This statement would only be blasphemy if it were false. Why not search for some evidence to support whether the claim is true or whether it is false? They did not even look for any evidence on this matter, but simply assumed that no one can make such a claim, and therefore condemned Him to death. What about bringing in Jairus as a witness; or someone from the wedding in Cana of Galilee; or the widow from Nain; or one of the ten lepers who was completely healed; or someone who ate of the loaves and the fish that fed over 5,000 men (not counting the women and children); or Lazarus himself who was readily available? No. They did not want witnesses who could corroborate the claim that Jesus is who He claimed to be. So, they had Him executed.

One way of looking at the resurrection is that it serves as God answering back to their false accusation of blasphemy. The high priest and other Jewish leaders had Him put to death, saying He blasphemed by calling Himself the Son of God, and so God answered back by raising Him from the dead. It is as though God is saying, "Oh, yes, He is the Son of God! Here He is, raised up from your unjust execution."

Once again, the Apostle Paul speaks to the matter:

> concerning his Son, who was descended from David according to the flesh and **was declared to be the Son of God** in power according to the Spirit of holiness **by his resurrection from the dead**, Jesus Christ our Lord, (Romans 1:3–4—emphasis added).

There is at least one more thing that the resurrection means. It was mentioned earlier that Jesus died to save people from their sins. The resurrection serves as proof that God accepts the sacrifice and justifies those who believe in His Son, Jesus Christ. To justify, simply put, means to have all the requirements of God's law fulfilled in your case. The penalty for your sins is paid in full and you are, legally speaking, right with God. Speaking of Abraham, Paul writes:

> No unbelief made him waver concerning the promise of God, but he grew strong in his faith as he gave glory to God, fully convinced that God was able to do what he had promised. That is why his faith was "counted to him as righteousness." But the words "it was counted to him" were not written for his sake alone, but for ours also. It will be counted to us who believe in him who raised from the dead Jesus our Lord, who was delivered up for our trespasses and raised for our justification (Romans 4:20–25).

This passage explains how God counted Abraham as righteous because he believed God's promise. It goes on to say that God will also count each one of us as righteous, if we have the same kind of faith that Abraham had, and points out that this faith includes knowing and believing that Jesus is Lord; that He was delivered up for our trespasses; and was raised from the dead for our justification. By the way, when God counts you as righteous, you are righteous, because God cannot lie.

To sum up, the resurrection is central to the Christian faith for at least these reasons: it demonstrates that Jesus has the power to impart eternal life; it declares forever that He is the Son of God; and demonstrates that those who believe in Him are justified before God.

How to Have Eternal Life

Many people actively pursue physical fitness. There are treadmills, jogging/walking trails, and memberships to fitness centers. All of this is good, but an even more important question is what are we doing to be spiritually fit? If you take care of yourself physically, you may postpone death, but you will not stop it. How do we prepare for death itself? It seems to me that death is the most significant problem facing mankind. Is there a cure for death?

Jesus said there is, and that He is it.

Truly, truly, I say to you, whoever believes has eternal life. I am the bread of life. Your fathers ate the manna in the wilderness, and they died. This is the bread that comes down from heaven, so that one may eat of it and not die. I am the living bread that came down from heaven. If anyone eats of this bread, he will live forever. And the bread that I will give for the life of the world is my flesh (John 6:47–51).

Jesus here contrasts meeting one's physical needs with meeting one's spiritual and eternal needs and claims to be the source of eternal life for everyone who puts their faith in Him.

In their various epistles, His apostles have explained how this works in greater detail. Paul, for example, writes:

… if you confess with your mouth that Jesus is Lord and believe in your heart that God raised Him from the dead, you will be saved. For with the heart one believes and is justified, and with the mouth one confesses and is saved. For the Scripture says, "Everyone who believes in him will not be put to shame." For there is no distinction between Jew and Greek; for the same Lord is Lord of all, bestowing his riches on all who call on him. For "everyone who calls on the name of the Lord will be saved" (Romans 10:9–13).

In the verse above, the Apostle explains that when anyone has enough faith in Jesus to believe that He is Lord; that He has been raised from the dead; to confess this; and to call on His name for salvation; then they will be saved. Being saved in this context means to be saved from eternal punishment from having sinned against God. The result is eternal life through Jesus Christ in His name.

Paul then describes the chain of events that leads to someone being saved in this way:

> How then will they call on him in whom they have not believed? And how are they to believe in him of whom they have never heard? And how are they to hear without someone preaching? And how are they to preach unless they are sent? As it is written, "How beautiful are the feet of those who preach the good news!" (Romans 10:14–15).

Here we see a clear sequence of things that must take place to bring someone to the point where they stop, turn from their own selfish ways (called repentance), and call on the name of the Lord to be saved from the penalty of having sinned. If we look at the passage from the bottom up, we get the picture. First, someone who already knows the good news from God is sent; then the sent person encounters people who do not know the good news; next, the one sent proclaims the good news; the ones who don't know it hear the message; if they have faith in the truthfulness and the goodness of God, they will unite the message from God with faith in their heart. In other words, they will believe what they hear concerning the good news; if they believe what they hear, then they will call on the name of the Lord to be saved from the penalty for having sinned against God. While not mentioned in this passage, other passages (such as 1 Peter 3:21, Acts 22:16, and Acts 2:38) point out that in association with calling on His name, one is baptized in water in the name of the Lord. The promise of God is that whoever calls on the name of the Lord will be saved, and to be saved is to have eternal life. This eternal life only comes in the name of Jesus Christ.

Summing it up

Even though Jesus knew that His dear friends would be greatly distressed by His arrest, humiliating torture, and unjust death, He still allowed it to happen because He saw ahead to the long-term end game, and knew that what He would be accomplishing would be more than well worth it. It would purchase salvation of the entire human race.

Once again, it is clear that while God allowed Mary, Martha, and Lazarus to experience a weighty loss; nevertheless, He restored their fortunes infinitely beyond what they were in the beginning, through the resurrection of Jesus Christ.

Chapter 20

The Message of Hope

M any readers are familiar with the following verse:

> "A voice was heard in Ramah, weeping and loud lamentation,
>
> Rachel weeping for her children; she refused to be comforted, because they are no more" (Matthew 2:18).

Matthew quotes this verse in response to King Herod the Great's horrible deed of destroying all the male children age two and younger in Bethlehem and the surrounding region. Matthew writes, "Then was fulfilled what was spoken by the prophet Jeremiah:" (Matthew 2:17). Then he quotes the verse.

How the words were fulfilled is an amazing story. This verse is presented as a message of hope, and not just a lamentation. How so? The answer to that question will be the focus of this chapter.

Herod in Action

To properly understand, we must first review the flow of events that led up to Herod's brutal action. Often, we hear this story related at Christmastime, as it deals with the birth of Jesus Christ. Magi (sometimes called the Wise Men) came to Jerusalem from the east and began to inquire, "Where is He who has been born King of the Jews? For we saw His star in the east and have come to worship Him" (Matthew 2:2 NASB).

The inquiry troubled Herod and all Jerusalem as well (Matthew

2:3 NASB). Herod was troubled because he had been given the title "King of the Jews" by the Roman senate (Josephus, p. 565). He was no doubt thinking, *Hey! Why are they looking for some baby to be the King of the Jews? I'm the King of the Jews!! This is not my baby!* He balked at the thought of a competitor.

Why was all Jerusalem troubled? Because of the simple fact that when Herod was displeased, everybody was on edge. They knew he was capable of becoming extremely volatile and wielded enough power for such moods to be deadly.

Herod concluded this "King of the Jews" must be the Jewish Messiah. He then inquired of the Jewish scribes to learn where the Messiah was to be born, to which they responded, "In Bethlehem of Judea ..." (Matthew 2:5 NASB). Calling in the magi, he instructed them to go to Bethlehem, and feigning recognition of the new king, said, "Go and search carefully for the Child; and when you have found *Him*, report to me, so that I too may come and worship Him" (Matthew 2:8 NASB).

The magi found the baby Jesus in Bethlehem, worshiped Him, and presented Him with the ever-famous gifts of gold, frankincense, and myrrh (Matthew 2:9–11 NASB). Instead of reporting back to King Herod, however, God warned them in a dream to return to their own country by another route (Matthew 2:12 NASB).

The Lord then sent an angel to Joseph who warned him to take his family, flee the area, and go to Egypt for a time (Matthew 2:13 NASB).

Once Herod figured out that the magi were not coming back, he became furious:

> Then when Herod saw that he had been tricked by the magi, he became very enraged, and sent *men* and killed all the boys who were in Bethlehem and all its vicinity, who were two years old or under, according to the time which he had determined from the magi (Matthew 2:16 NASB).

Now comes the verse with which we began this chapter:

Then was fulfilled what was spoken by the prophet Jeremiah:

"A voice was heard in Ramah, weeping and loud lamentation,

Rachel weeping for her children; she refused to be comforted, because they are no more" (Matthew 2:17–18).

I began this chapter by stating this quote is intended by Matthew to be a message of hope for his readers, and not just a lamentation. It is a lamentation, but even more so, it resonates as a message of hope.

The people of Bethlehem, and Matthew's readers were apt to have been wondering how could the Lord allow this horrible tragedy to occur? He obviously saw it coming. First, being God, He knows all things. Additionally, He warned the magi, and warned Joseph, but what about the other residents of Bethlehem? Why were they not somehow protected? Imagine what it must have been like for the young families in Bethlehem, and the surrounding region, to have their small children ripped from their arms and destroyed in this way. Why was it allowed to happen?

The answer that I offer is, *I do not know.* I do not know what warnings God may have given to the other people. Were there warnings that were ignored? Were the people open to listening to God's voice? Again, I do not claim to know. What I do know is that God knows more than I do, and I know that His nature is good. I also know that when His people go through intense pain and suffering, He has a message of hope for them.

The Message to the Captives

There are a few things here we need to understand. First, Bethlehem and Ramah are not the same town. Bethlehem is located approximately five miles south of Jerusalem in the land of Judah, while Ramah is about five miles north of Jerusalem in the land allotted to the tribe of Benjamin (Myers, pp. 143 and 871). Why then, does Matthew refer to a passage that has Rachel weeping for her children, when the children of Bethlehem are descendants of Judah, who was a son of Leah?

The passage quoted in Matthew 2:17–18 is from Jeremiah,

Chapter 31. To understand why Matthew applies it here, we must become familiar with the passage's surrounding verses and its original context. As we saw in previous chapters, God had warned the people of Israel not to worship false gods, but to faithfully obey Him. Yet generation after generation refused to listen, and so the Lord finally sent punishment upon them. The prophet Hosea predicted that destruction would come upon the lands of Benjamin and Ephraim, including the town of Ramah (Hosea 5:8–9). In the ninth year of Zedekiah (about 588 BC), King of Judah, King Nebuchadnezzar of Babylon, marched on Jerusalem to destroy it. After an 18-month long siege, the wall was breached, and Jerusalem fell. The city was burned and reduced to rubble, including the beloved temple which King Solomon had built centuries earlier. Many people were killed. Details of this event are told in Jeremiah, Chapter 39; 2 Kings, Chapter 25; and 2 Chronicles, Chapter 36. 2 Chronicles, for example, says:

> Yet the LORD, the God of their fathers, sent *word* to them again and again by His messengers, because He had compassion on His people and on His dwelling place; but they *continually* mocked the messengers of God, despised His words, and scoffed at His prophets, until the wrath of the LORD rose against His people, until there was no remedy.
>
> So He brought up against them the king of the Chaldeans who killed their young men with the sword in the house of their sanctuary, and had no compassion on young man or virgin, old man or frail; He handed *them* all over to him (2 Chronicles 36:15–17 NASB).

After Jerusalem fell, the people of Judah who had survived the destruction were gathered and assembled in Ramah in preparation for their deportation to Babylon (Harrison, p. 159). It is here, in this context, that Jeremiah describes Rachel as weeping and refusing to be comforted because so many of her children had been destroyed. God's people, gathered in Ramah, were going through days of dark pain. The majority had been killed, and most of those who did survive were being sent to captivity in a strange land; only a few of the poorest of the poor were left behind to tend vineyards and farm (2 Kings 25:12).

It was at this time that the Lord gave Jeremiah a message to deliver to the surviving captives. It was a message of hope. The message is recorded in Jeremiah, Chapters 30 and 31. According to biblical commentator, R. K. Harrison, these chapters form part of a section frequently referred to as the "Book of Consolation" and interrupt an otherwise somber portion of Jeremiah's work (Harrison, p. 133). To the captives the Lord promised that the people of God would one day return and their fortunes would be restored.

> I will build you again and you will be rebuilt,
> Virgin of Israel!
> You will take up your tambourines again,
> And go out to the dances of the revelers.
> Again you will plant vineyards
> On the hills of Samaria;
> The planters will plant
> And will enjoy *the fruit* (Jeremiah 31:4–5 NASB).

And,

> This is what the LORD says:
> "A voice is heard in Ramah,
> Lamenting *and* bitter weeping,
> Rachel is weeping for her children.
> She refuses to be comforted for her children,
> Because they are no more."
>
> This is what the LORD says:
> "Restrain your voice from weeping
> And your eyes from tears;
> For your work will be rewarded," declares the LORD,
> "And they will return from the land of the enemy.
> "There is hope for your future," declares the LORD,
> "And *your* children will return to their own territory."
> (Jeremiah 31:15–17 NASB)

The days were coming when the weeping would be replaced with joy, gladness, and merrymaking as the captives return to their homeland again. The weeping of Rachel would be restrained because her children would return.

The Promise of the Real Deal

People need hope. Hope to the soul is as air and water are to the body. Without it, one loses heart and despairs. The captives of Judah had begun to lose hope and had begun to complain against God for all the trouble that had come upon them. They created a proverb that said, "… 'The fathers have eaten sour grapes, and the children's teeth are set on edge'" (Jeremiah 31:29). That is like saying, "Our ancestors did the dirty deeds, but we are the ones paying for it." The lie of the ages was rearing its ugly head again. This proverb was a way of denying their own guilt and accusing God of unfairness. It is natural to look for someone other than ourselves to blame when we are suffering.

The Lord was displeased with the proverb, and Ezekiel records that He commanded the captives to stop using it (Ezekiel 18:1–3). Yet He did more than simply command them to stop using it; He gave them hope. In addition to the hope that their descendants would one day return with gladness, God gave them an even weightier promise. He promised to establish a new covenant, a better covenant, an eternal, life-giving covenant.

> "Behold, days are coming," declares the LORD, "when I will make a new covenant with the house of Israel and the house of Judah, not like the covenant which I made with their fathers in the day I took them by the hand to bring them out of the land of Egypt, My covenant which they broke, although I was a husband to them," declares the LORD. "For this is the covenant which I will make with the house of Israel after those days," declares the LORD: "I will put My law within them and write it on their heart; and I will be their God, and they shall be My people. They will not teach again, each one his neighbor and each one his brother, saying, 'Know the LORD,' for they will all know Me, from the least of them to the greatest of them," declares the LORD, "for I will forgive their wrongdoing, and their sin I will no longer remember" (Jeremiah 31:31–34 NASB).

This covenant was not to be like the one God brought through Moses. That covenant had been broken by them and by their ancestors. They worshiped other gods, which they were commanded not to do, and they sinned, both they and their fathers. The reason so many had been killed, and the survivors had become captives, was because they had broken the old covenant repeatedly.

This was not to be just any new covenant; this was The New Covenant. This was to be a covenant in which God, Himself would do the heavy lifting. He would not just write His law on tablets for them to know and obey, but would write it on their hearts, thus changing their nature. He would empower them. He would be their God, they would all know Him, and their sins would be forgiven and remembered no more. The book of Hebrews explains that in the old covenant, the animal sacrifices did not bring actual forgiveness, but were a mere shadow of it (see Hebrews, Chapter 10). In this New Covenant, forgiveness would be the real deal. This is the covenant that the Messiah would institute, this is the covenant that would make eternal life a reality. They were going through intense pain and grief; the day was coming when such would be no more. Life would be eternal, their relationship with God would be completely healed, and pain would be gone forever. It was real, and it was coming. This gave them the hope they needed.

The promised Holy Spirit

In the promise of the New Covenant, Jeremiah mentions that God would write His law on the hearts of His people. In other words, there would be a change in their heart and in their nature. This is brought about by the gift of the Holy Spirit. As one is baptized in the name of Jesus Christ, one is promised the gift of the Holy Spirit (Acts 2:38–39). Once the Holy Spirit is given, His presence brings tremendous benefits into the life of the believer. He brings a new fellowship with God and His people (1 John 1:3 and Philippians 2:1); He brings comfort; He brings counsel (John 14:26); and He empowers the believer to walk in accord with His counsel and wisdom (Ephesians 3:16–17). In this way, God not only shows the believer His wisdom, but also empowers him or her to walk in it. These blessings are realized in the New Covenant which the Lord promised through Jeremiah's prophecy.

Back to Bethlehem

As Matthew relates what occurred in Bethlehem, he is writing of a people who were suffering weighty pain and grief, as did the Hebrew captives of a previous generation. His message concerning them is the same as that which Jeremiah had given to the Hebrew captives. There is hope. During all this tragedy, there is still hope. Matthew originally wrote to Hebrew Christians (Tasker, pp. 11–12) who would have been familiar with Jeremiah's message, and the mention of Rachel weeping in Ramah would bring the whole message to mind. This was not just about Rachel weeping, but about God's promise of a hope that would bring restoration. Even though pain, suffering, and death are experienced on earth, God promised through Jeremiah to bring a New Covenant in which His people (all who call on His name) would experience the forgiveness of sins and a genuine restored relationship with Him, the result of which is eternal life. The child born in Bethlehem in connection with these events came to establish the New Covenant, and thus fulfill Jeremiah's prophecy.

In Summary

In the days of the fall of Jerusalem, the people gathered at Ramah were given a promise of an eternal hope that would help them get through the difficult times. Yet now that the New Covenant has been instituted by Jesus Christ, Christians have this same promise and more. We have the eternal hope, but we also have the genuine forgiveness of sins, which makes reconciliation with God possible; and we have God's law written in our hearts by the work of His Holy Spirit, and by gift of the Holy Spirit, we are not only given the wisdom to navigate painful and difficult times, but the power to walk in that wisdom, as well.

❧ Chapter 21 ☙

Loving God

The Greatest Commandment and a Great Promise

In the Word of God, there is a commandment that is called by Jesus the greatest commandment. It is the commandment to love God with all of one's heart, all of one's soul, all of one's mind, and all of one's strength (Mark 12:28–30).

To some, this might sound like a tall order. They may wonder, *How can anyone love like that?* The truth is, however, that God does not leave people to do this on their own. Love begins with God and then it flows to those people who are responsive to Him.

The Apostle John states that love begins with God:

Beloved, let us love one another, for love is from God, and whoever loves has been born of God and knows God. Anyone who does not love does not know God, because God is love. In this the love of God was made manifest among us, that God sent his only Son into the world, so that we might live through him. In this is love, not that we have loved God but that he loved us and sent his Son to be the propitiation for our sins (1 John 4:7–10).

He also wrote, "We love because he first loved us" (1 John 4:19).

John is explaining that our love is a response to the fact that God has first loved us. When we fully comprehend the extent and the depth of God's love for us, and the action He has taken to demonstrate that love, it draws from us a response to love Him in return.

While our love for God is a response on our part to understanding how much He loves us, there is more to it than that. God not only takes the initiative to love us first, but He also empowers us to love, as well. Paul explains that one reason Christians have hope while suffering is because "God's love has been poured into our hearts through the Holy Spirit who has been given to us" (Romans 5:5). Couple this with a statement Jesus made and we begin to get the picture.

> On the last day of the feast, the great day, Jesus stood up and cried out, "If anyone thirsts, let him come to me and drink. Whoever believes in me, as the Scripture has said, 'Out of his heart will flow rivers of living water.'" Now this he said about the Spirit, whom those who believed in him were to receive, for as yet the Spirit had not been given, because Jesus was not yet glorified (John 7:37–39).

Since Jesus has now been glorified (His death, resurrection, and ascension to heaven), the promised indwelling presence of the Holy Spirit is given to those who believe in Him (Acts 2:38–39). One of the things the Spirit does as He indwells a person is produce the springs of living water mentioned by Jesus, which then flow out from the heart of this person. He dwells in the believer and continually pours God's love into their heart, and this becomes a spring of living water that fills the person so that they, in turn, are pouring out love for God and for other people. This is an ongoing process. The believer is open to the Lord's workmanship, and the Lord continues to pour His love into their heart. One must be receptive to God, however, for this to take place. Even an almighty God cannot give to a person who has no capacity to receive (Lewis, *A Grief Observed*, p. 54). It would be like trying to pour water into a cup that still has the lid fastened tight. One must be open to God for this process to work.

So, we see that loving God is the greatest commandment, and God assists us and empowers us to keep it.

Next, we need to look at one of the most powerful promises that God makes to those who keep the greatest commandment. The promise is found in Paul's letter to the Romans. It reads, "And we know that for those who love God all things work together for good, for those who are called according to his purpose" (Romans 8:28).

Think of that. If you love God, you are called according to His purpose, and everything in your life will somehow work together for good. That means every success; every failure; every glad moment; every sad moment; every blessing that is given; and every treasure that is lost. All the events in your life work together to form a tapestry that is guaranteed by God to have a good outcome. We even know what that outcome will be; you will be "conformed to the image of His Son" (Romans 8:29). No event, whether seemly good or seemingly bad, is wasted; God uses it all for His purpose, and His purpose for you is good.

Grieve not the Holy Spirit

In his letter to the Ephesians, Paul gives his readers a very interesting exhortation. He says, "And do not grieve the Holy Spirit of God, by whom you were sealed for the day of redemption" (Ephesians 4:30). By making this statement, Paul is revealing something very important about God. He can be grieved by people. God, who is all knowing (Psalm 139) and all powerful (Luke 1:37), has chosen to create people in such a way that we are capable of making choices and taking actions that grieve Him. He created us in a manner that makes Himself vulnerable to pain. Who made Him do this? The answer, of course, is no one (at least, no one outside of Himself).

The lie of the ages implies that God is selfish, but it is my belief that a self-serving all-powerful being would not create other beings in a way that would leave Himself vulnerable to any inconvenience, including experiencing pain. Grief is painful. Grief is a form of pain experienced when one loses or is separated from someone or something they love. If God can be grieved by humans, in my view it demonstrates that He loves us.

We must now think about atheists for a little bit. This is necessary, at this point, because we are addressing the topic of loving God, and atheism is the opposite of loving God. I think you will see what I mean as we move forward.

The testimony of God is that there is enough evidence available to all people everywhere to leave them without excuse if they do not honor Him as God and give Him thanks for creating all things.

> For what can be known about God is plain to them, because God has shown it to them. For his invisible attributes, namely, his eternal power and divine nature, have been clearly perceived, ever since the creation of the world, in the things that have been made. So they are without excuse. For although they knew God, they did not honor him as God or give thanks to him, but they became futile in their thinking, and their foolish hearts were darkened (Romans 1:19–21).

Here we see what can be called an external witness to the reality of God as Creator. This witness consists of the things He has made. I call this an external witness because it is outside of oneself. It involves all the things that exist in the world, many of which are detectable with the human senses and the tools of science. This statement was made by the Apostle Paul nearly two thousand years ago, and yet in modern times, the advances of science serve to demonstrate its truthfulness even more clearly. The more man observes things like molecular structure, cell structure, biological processes, and astrophysics, the more he can see the intricate design and beauty of the whole creation. The evidence declares that there is a designer, and the evidence is present in the physical world for all people to see. This is what I mean by an external witness.

The Word of God also claims that there is an internal witness in every person.

> For when Gentiles, who do not have the law, by nature do what the law requires, they are a law to themselves, even though they do not have the law. They show that the work of the law is written on their hearts, while their conscience also bears witness, and their conflicting thoughts accuse or even excuse them on that day when, according to my gospel, God judges the secrets of men by Christ Jesus (Romans 2:14–16).

Here the Apostle describes a law that is written in the hearts of people even if they do not have a written copy of God's Word. There is something within them that tells them of God and of His moral requirements. This is the internal witness in each person.

To claim that there is no God, a person must suppress both the internal witness in his/her own heart, and the external witness built into all the visible creation. Paul says they are suppressing the truth in unrighteousness (Romans 1:18). It is to pretend God is *not* there, when the person knows He *is* there. This is the opposite of love.

Just imagine, for a minute, if you did this to any human person you know. Suppose a friend sends a message to you, and you ignore it. The friend calls you and you do not answer; or they come to your home and knock on the door, knowing you are there, but you refuse to answer. What if this friend entered a room in which you are present, but you do not greet them, or even look at them; instead, you pretend they are not there. This person would be deeply hurt and offended. This is what atheists are doing to God. It is the opposite of loving Him.

The sad reality is that when people treat God this way, the promise of Romans 8:28 is not guaranteed. God does not stop loving them, but until they are willing to take the lid off their cup, they are not able to receive many of the blessings that could be theirs. The pain and grief they encounter in life seem futile, the lie of the ages settles in, and many descend into despair. How tragic this is; the despair is completely avoidable.

By contrast, the Christian is promised that God's love is poured into their heart, and their hope in the Lord's promises will not disappoint them (Romans 5:5).

Nothing can separate the child of God from His love.

For I am sure that neither death nor life, nor angels nor rulers, nor things present nor things to come, nor powers, nor height nor depth, nor anything else in all creation, will be able to separate us from the love of God in Christ Jesus our Lord (Romans 8:38–39).

All the things mentioned in this passage have one thing in common; they are in the realm of created things. They are not God. God exists outside of the set of things called "anything else in all creation." He is the Creator. Love begins with Him. The created things and created powers cannot stop God's love. The creation has no power to stop the Creator from doing anything that is His will to do, and it is His will to love. Once you open your heart to be filled with the love of God, He will pour it into you from outside of the creation, and there is no power in all creation that can stop this from happening. Even suffering, grief, and death cannot stop God's love. Jesus Christ has already demonstrated that He is greater than death itself.

Chapter 22

What About You?

Up to this point, we have investigated the example of Mary, Martha, and Lazarus of Bethany in Judea, and have seen that they asked the Lord for help in their time of need. His coming to help them was delayed. At first, they did not understand why, but then they saw that His intentions for them had been good all along. He briefly took them deeper into grief, but brought them to a result that had permanent benefits which far outweighed the temporary grief.

Next, we studied other examples from the biblical text. There were Abraham, Job, Joseph, and the others whom God walked through very difficult things. In the Scriptures there are many other examples of God working in this way in the lives of people. There were Moses, David, Jeremiah, and Daniel, just to name a few, but time does not allow me to dig deeply into every case. To some of you, however, all these examples seem so distant. They happened a long time ago.

What about you? What is your situation? What is going on right now that has you wondering if God still works in the same way today? What are His intentions for you?

The good news is that God's nature is unchanging (Hebrews 13:8), and He does not show any partiality (Romans 2:11). If we, today, show the same kind of faith that these biblical people demonstrated, then God will deal with us as He did them.

He may solve your problem right now. The Scriptures tell us to present our requests before Him, to ask in prayer with thanksgiving when we have a need, and to expect results (Philippians 4:6–7). The

Bible teaches us to put aside fear, and to know that God is our ever-present help in time of trouble (Psalm 46:1–2).

Yet, if He does seem to delay in resolving whatever it is that you are facing, remember Mary, Martha, Lazarus, and the other biblical examples. The Lord always comes through. It may be now, it may be later, but He will not fail. Even if you must wait until the eternal kingdom is ushered in, that does not mean God failed or did not provide your answer. The eternal kingdom is more real than our present world, and there we will find many answers that seem to have evaded us in this present life. God will always come through for the one who calls on His name (Romans 10:13).

I do not know when or how He will choose to come through for you, but I know that His intentions for you are good. He may be delaying so that He can do more, not less. He may be testing your faith, the way He tested Abraham's. He may be using you to silence the accusations of the enemy, the way He used Job. He may be working to bring about a result that will save other people's lives, the way He did with Joseph. He may be working to show who He is to someone who has great power and influence, the way He worked through Shadrach, Meshach, and Abednego.

I do not know His specific plan for you, but I know that His intentions are good, His love is real, and His nature is unchanging. He wants you to glorify His name in your situation, whatever it is (1 Corinthians 10:31). He invites you to call upon Him, and to draw near to Him. He wants a perfect and intimate fellowship with you. Sometimes, even though He loves you—no, sometimes, **because** He loves you, He will delay. He may first lead you deeper into grief. Yet this is temporary, and the result will be better than you could have imagined. He will restore your fortunes.

Remember that He is working in realms that we do not always see. Just like with Job, the things we go through can have a huge impact in the spiritual realm. Other people, as well, are affected by the things we go through. You do not always know who is watching you and your situation. When Nebuchadnezzar saw how the Lord dealt with Shadrach, Meshach, and Abednego, it literally changed his view of the living God. Others may eventually come to have faith in Jesus Christ because of what they see in your example, as you walk through difficult times.

God desires for each one of us to grow into a deeper trust; a stronger faith; a closer walk with Him; an unwavering hope; and a greater love. Keep the faith and maintain your hope in the Lord.

Be Courageous

In 2011, Kendrick Brothers Productions released a film entitled *Courageous*. The movie follows a deputy sheriff named Adam Mitchell and his family. He has a wife named Victoria, a fifteen-year-old son named Dylan, and a nine-year-old daughter named Emily. During the events of the movie, Emily is suddenly killed in an auto accident while being driven to a birthday party by some friends of the family. The accident is caused by a drunk driver. The Mitchell family is devastated by the unexpected tragedy. After the funeral is over and all the friends and relatives have left, there is a scene in which Victoria comes to Adam, and says, "Make sense of this for me." She then cries out, "Why? Why?"—wondering aloud why their daughter was killed and "that drunk" is still alive (*Courageous*, 48:23). Adam does not have an answer for her. He then laments that he had not been a better father. Victoria reminds him that he is still a father. Adam then goes to his son, Dylan, and attempts to talk to him, but his comforting efforts seem to fall flat as his relationship with Dylan has been a bit strained up to this point.

Adam decides to go see Pastor Rogers, the minister of the church their family attends, to seek some advice.

He confesses, "I can't make sense of anything, you know? I guess I kinda' feel like I'm in the dark. And I want to be there for Victoria, but my emotions are all over the place. So I don't know what to do."

Pastor Rogers gently reminds him that the Lord is the One who carries us through the grieving process, but that it takes time. "It takes time for healing," he says.

To which Adam responds, "Healing?"

Pastor Rogers says, "I've heard many people say, who've lost a loved one, that in some ways, it's like learning to live with an amputation. You do heal, but you're never the same. But I would also say that those who go through this and trust in the Lord, discover a comfort and an intimacy with God that most people never experience."

"I want to trust Him. I just don't understand what He's doing," responds Adam.

"Well, He doesn't promise an explanation," says Pastor Rogers, "but He does promise to walk with us through the pain. And the hard choice for you is whether or not you're going to be angry for the time you didn't have with her, or grateful for the time you did have" (*Courageous*, 52:48–54:20).

This line from Pastor Rogers strikes me as being very profound. When pain hits hard, when it all appears completely unjust, and when the answers are nowhere to be found, can we remember to give thanks for the blessings that are still present before us? Will we focus on what we do not have, or be grateful for what we do have? If we only think on the pain of what has been lost, we can miss the joy of the blessings that are still present.

Adam responded to Pastor Rogers' comment by saying that he did not want to be angry. He then resolved to pursue the will of God, and to seek out how to become the best husband and father that he could be, with God's help. It does take courage to do this.

We would do well to imitate Adam's attitude. When trouble comes, we need to reject the lie of the ages; have the courage to seek God's will; focus on our many present blessings; and learn to give thanks in all circumstances (Ephesians 5:20 and Colossians 3:17).

We Do Not Always Know Why

The night Jesus shared in His final meal with his disciples before being arrested, He did something that was very unusual for a leader and a teacher. It caught His disciples completely off guard. He washed their feet.

Now before the Feast of the Passover, when Jesus knew that his hour had come to depart out of this world to the Father, having loved his own who were in the world, he loved them to the end. During supper, when the devil had already put it into the heart of Judas Iscariot, Simon's son, to betray him, Jesus, knowing that the Father had given all things into his hands, and that he had come from God and was going back to God, rose from supper. He laid aside his outer garments, and taking a towel, tied it around his waist. Then he poured water into a basin and began to wash the disciples' feet and to wipe them with the towel that was wrapped around him (John 13:1–5).

You can just feel John's astonishment as he writes his account of what happened. He works hard to convince the reader that Jesus knew what He was doing. He tells us, Jesus knew his hour had come; He knew that Judas was already planning to betray Him; He knew that God had given all things into His hand; He knew that He had come from God; He knew He was going back to God; and He loved His disciples. He was aware of who He was; where He had come from; and where He was going to. He was completely aware of His rights, privileges, and position. He was even aware of Judas' intentions, and yet He washed his feet, too.

This task was such a disgusting thing to have to do, it was often relegated to a servant (*The Eerdman's Bible Dictionary,* p. 390). The disciples were wondering, *Why is He doing this, when He is the Lord?* Peter was so taken aback that, at first, he hesitated to allow Jesus to wash his feet (John 13:6).

Jesus' response to Peter's objection is what I want to focus on here.

Jesus answered him, "What I am doing you do not understand now, but afterward you will understand" (John 13:7).

This is what we need to understand. The Lord knows things we do not know. He understands things that we do not understand. Some things are things He is not willing to explain right now, but later, we will understand better.

When you go through a thing that makes no sense to you whatsoever, and the pain is more than seems fair for anyone to bear, hear the words of the Lord saying to you, "What I am doing you do not understand now, but afterward you will understand." If you reject the lie of the ages, and persevere in the love of God, trusting that He has your best interests at heart, it will one day work together for good (Romans 8:28).

The time will come when you understand.

The Last Enemy Defeated

During our life on earth, we as people suffer many things, but the greatest and final enemy of the human race is death. Mankind has not and never will discover a cure for death on his own. God, however, has a cure. His cure is Jesus Christ.

> ... when He has abolished all rule and all authority and power. For He must reign until He has put all enemies under His feet. The last enemy that will be abolished is death (1 Corinthians 15:24–26, NASB).

> And I heard a loud voice from the throne, saying, "Behold, the tabernacle of God is among the people, and He will dwell among them, and they shall be His people, and God Himself will be among them, and He will wipe away every tear from their eyes; and there will no longer be *any* death; there will no longer be *any* mourning, or crying, or pain; the first things have passed away" (Revelation 21:3–4, NASB).

The day is coming when all sickness, pain, and even death itself, will be no more. The fact that this promise is for a day in the future does not mean that it is not real. It will come. This hope is just as certain, and just as real as the history that has already occurred. Jesus Christ, through His atoning death and resurrection, has defeated for all time the last enemy.

Do not Miss Out on Glorifying God

One of the main points I hope every reader of this book will take away after having read it is that glorifying God is something you do not want to miss. While in this present world, we cannot measure the true weight of glorifying God. I am convinced that it is huge. Pursue this with everything you have. If it means giving up some pleasure, pursue it. If it means denying yourself (and it does), pursue it. If it means going against the grain, pursue it. Even when it involves suffering, pursue glorifying Him just the same. Learn from the example of Paul. He gave his all when it came to glorifying God.

If you are a child of God, you will be called to suffer with Christ.

The Spirit himself bears witness with our spirit that we are children of God, and if children, then heirs—heirs of God and fellow heirs with Christ, provided we suffer with him in order that we may also be glorified with him (Romans 8:16–17).

Is it worth suffering a little while here on earth, that we may be heirs of God? Of course, it is!

Just remember, the trouble is temporary. God will restore your fortunes. He does have your best interests at heart. And say, with the Apostle Paul,

"... I consider that the sufferings of this present time are not worth comparing with the glory that is to be revealed to us" (Romans 8:18).

Sources

Andersen, Francis I. *Job: An Introduction and Commentary*. InterVarsity Press, Leicester, England and Downers Grove, Illinois, 1981. From the Tyndale Old Testament Commentaries, D.J. Wiseman, General Editor.

Baptism Site "Bethany Beyond the Jordan" (Al-Maghtas)—UNESCO World Heritage Centre. UNESCO. https://whc.unesco.org/en/list/1446. Retrieved 10 April 2020.

Cottrell, Jack. *What the Bible Says About God the Creator.* College Press Publishing Company, Joplin, Missouri, 1983.

Cottrell, Jack. *What the Bible Says About God The Redeemer.* College Press Publishing Company, Joplin, Missouri, 1987.

Courageous. Directed by Alex Kendrick, TriStar Pictures and Sherwood Pictures in association with Provident Films and Affirm Films, a Kendrick Brothers Production, 2011, DVD 2012.

Easton, M. G. *Illustrated Bible Dictionary*. Harvest House Publishers, Revised Edition, 1978.

Eggerichs, Dr. Emerson. *Love and Respect: The Love She Most Desires, The Respect He Desperately Needs*. Thomas Nelson, 2004.

"Evaluations of Nominations of Cultural and Mixed Properties to the World Heritage List: ICOMOS Report" (PDF). UNESCO Organization. 2015. pp. 49–50. Retrieved 10 April 2020.

Foster, R. C. *Studies in the Life of Christ*. Baker Book House, Fourth Printing, 1982.

Harrison, R. K., B.D., M.Th., PhD. *Jeremiah and Lamentations—An Introduction and Commentary.* InterVarsity Press, Downers Grove, Illinois, 1973.

Interlinear Greek-English New Testament—Numerically Coded to Strong's Exhaustive Concordance, White, Donald R., Editor. Baker Book House, Grand Rapids, Michigan, 3rd Printing, 1984.

Jones, Dr. Floyd Nolen, *The Chronology of the Old Testament: A return to the basics.* Master Books, Green Forest, AZ, 8th Printing, 2017.

Lewis, C. S. *A Grief Observed.* A Bantam Book/published by arrangement with The Seabury Press Inc., New York, NY, 7th printing, 1980.

Lewis, C. S. *The Weight of Glory and Other Addresses.* Revised and Expanded Edition, Edited, and with an Introduction by Walter Hooper, Collier Books, MacMillan Publishers Company, New York, 1980.

"Bring the Rain" Simpleville Music (ASCAP) / Wet As A Fish Music (ASCAP) / (admin at EssentialMusicPublishing.com (http://www.essentialmusicpublishing.com/)). All rights reserved. Used by permission.

Schaeffer, Francis A. *Genesis in Space and Time: The Flow of Biblical History.* InterVarsity Press, Downers Grove, Illinois, 1972.

The Constitution of the United States with the Declaration of Independence, Sterling Publishing Co. Inc. for the Fall River Press, New York, New York, 2012 edition.

Tasker, R. V. G., M.A., D.D. *The Gospel According to St. Matthew: An Introduction and Commentary.* InterVarsity Press, Leicester, England and William B. Eerdman's Publishing Company, Grand Rapids, Michigan, 1961, Reprinted 1983.

The Eerdman's Bible Dictionary. Myers, Allen C., Editor. Simpson, John W. Jr.; Frank, Philip A.; Jenney, Timothy P.; Vunderink, Ralph W.; Associate Editors. William B. Eerdman's Publishing Company, Grand Rapids, Michigan, 1987.

The ESV Archeology Study Bible, ESV Bible, Copyright 2017 by Crossway, Wheaton, Illinois.

The Works of Josephus: New Updated Edition, Complete and Unabridged in One Volume. Whiston, William, A.M. Translator. Hendrickson Publishers, Inc., 1987. Tenth Printing, 1995.

Vine, W. E., M.A. *An Expository Dictionary of New Testament Words—with their Precise Meanings for English Readers.* Fleming H. Revell Company, Old Tappan, New Jersey, 17th impression, 1966.

Taken from *A Survey of Israel's History* by Leon Wood. Copyright © 1982, Fifteenth printing by Leon Wood. Used by permission of Zondervan. www.zondervan.com.

www.ingramcontent.com/pod-product-compliance
Lightning Source LLC
Chambersburg PA
CBHW072346090426
42741CB00012B/2942